THE GOD OF
NEW
BEGINNINGS

THE GOD OF
NEW
BEGINNINGS

*Brief Insights
from Genesis and Exodus*

WILLIAM E. McCUMBER

 Beacon Hill Press of Kansas City
Kansas City, Missouri

Unless otherwise indicated, all Scripture quotations are from the *Revised Standard Version of the Bible* (RSV), copyrighted 1946, 1952, © 1971, 1973 by the Division of Christian Education of the National Council of the Churches of Christ in the U.S.A., and are used by permission.

Permission to quote from another copyrighted version of the Bible is acknowledged with appreciation:

The *New Revised Standard Version of the Bible* (NRSV), copyright © 1989, by the Division of Christian Education of the National Council of the Churches of Christ in the U.S.A.

The King James Version of the Bible is indicated by KJV.

10   9   8   7   6   5   4   3   2   1

Contents

1

In the Beginning

The majestic opening statement of the Bible never fails to intrigue and excite me.

> *In the beginning God created the heavens and the earth* (Gen. 1:1).

As someone long ago remarked, "How simple! How sublime! How satisfying!"

Simple indeed! It is a statement of origins that a child can read, yet no philosopher, theologian, or scientist can improve upon that statement.

Sublime indeed! It introduces us, not to blind chance or random force, but to the impenetrable mystery of the personal, almighty God.

Satisfying indeed! It satisfies the inquiring mind that seeks an adequate cause for the well-nigh infinity, complexity, and variety of effects throughout the universe. It satisfies the adoring heart that yearns to link its life and give its love to Someone who is great enough and good enough to invest that outpouring of life and love with eternal value.

I. "IN THE BEGINNING . . ."

No other theory of origins ever substituted for Gen. 1:1 makes sense if you posit a beginning. Only when we push back to some point that still falls short of the beginning can any other explanation command the respect of logic and faith. That some are unwilling to go back to the beginning says more about their religious unbelief than their scientific knowledge. When man is determined to be his own god, when he bows before his own intellect in willful pride, he can be expected to refuse to trace origins to the originating God.

II. "IN THE BEGINNING GOD . . ."

God, the indescribable, the unanalyzable, the incomprehensible, the uncontainable, is *there*. He can be named, but He cannot be proved. He can be confessed, but He cannot be measured, managed, or manipulated. He is eternal and sovereign. He is before all things; He is above all things. Nothing precedes Him, nothing succeeds Him, nothing preempts Him.

The Bible affirms God, it does not argue Him. God does not exist by the sufferance of the creature. He is not the end term of philosophical arguments. He is not the unreal projection of minds that flee their finitude and despair of their security. He simply *is*, always was, and ever shall be—whether we believe it or not.

People can deny Him. They can ignore Him. They can defy Him. They can pit their minds and hearts and wills against Him in rebellion, but they cannot escape Him! God is the Source, the purpose, and the goal of human existence. To buck that truth is to distort and pervert life, to render life less than truly human, and to court ultimate failure even in the midst of apparent success. For God is *there*, and we shall have to reckon with Him, like it or not.

III. "IN THE BEGINNING GOD CREATED . . ."

The God of the Bible is "the living God," the God who acts, who does things. He brings into existence, and main-

8

tains in existence, "the heavens and the earth." He created that which was not himself. He created that which was not necessary to himself. He willed that to exist as creation whose origin, reason, and future were not self-contained but could only have their meaning and value in relationship to the Creator.

So heaven and earth, and all that fills them, is an expression of God's *grace*, His turning toward that which is not himself to give it being and purpose. From "the beginning" God is the God of grace, whose love flows forth to that which is unnecessary to Him but for whom He is utterly necessary. He turns from himself, turns toward all else than himself, causing it to be, conferring order upon it, and investing it with goodness. What a God!

"The heavens and the earth" cannot exist without Him. He is prior to His creation, and He cannot be excluded from it. He is greater than His creation, and He cannot be contained within it. Rebellion has occurred. Man has fallen from the Creator's fellowship, involving all creation in his ruin. But the Creator's grace continues to embrace, to preserve, and to redeem His fallen creation.

God's love was not defeated by man's sin. Sin diminished man, not God! The opening statement of Genesis begins a story of divine activity on behalf of unworthy mankind, an activity whose heart is summed up in the apostolic declaration: "God was in Christ, reconciling the world unto himself" (2 Cor. 5:19, KJV). God came in Jesus Christ, who lived, died, and rose again—bearing sin, defeating death, and opening to us the gates of eternal life.

* * *

"In the beginning God created the heavens and the earth." Through time and eternity, therefore, His name be praised!

9

2

Adam Is Everyone

So God created man in his own image, in the image of God he created him; male and female he created them (Gen. 1:27).

Adam was an individual, the very first man. But Adam was also a corporate figure; Adam is you and me—everyone. His story is our story, and the story can be summed up in three related words: Made, unmade, and remade.

I. The making of Adam was the work of God

"So God created man in his own image." All that is meant by "the image of God" has challenged and bested the minds of theologians across the centuries. We can understand a part of what it means from the context.

To be like God is to *exercise power.* God said to His creature man, "Have dominion" (v. 28), and made him lord over animal and plant life.

To be like God is to *live in relationships.* We read, "Male and female he created them." Man is a "them," never complete as an individual, but finding his identity and purpose in life with others.

To be like God is to have a *capacity for communion with God.* God's first recorded action toward man was to speak to him: "God blessed them, and God said unto them . . ." (v. 28, KJV). God's first gifts to man were speech and language. Man shares his earth origin with the animals, but his capacity for communion with God as a speech partner marks man off from the animals as unique.

While you and I were not fashioned directly by God, as was Adam, nevertheless we have our life as a gift from God, and we bear His image, though in a damaged form.

A damaged form! That brings us to chapter 2 in the story of Adam.

II. THE UNMAKING OF ADAM WAS THE WORK OF SIN

Adam disobeyed God, and the image of God was marred. Indeed, it was all but destroyed. Adam's sin was more than simply eating an apple—or whatever the forbidden fruit was. The forbidden fruit, a restriction upon human freedom, symbolized the truth that man is not God. Man is *lord over the earth*, but he is *steward under God*. Adam wanted lordship without stewardship, privileges without responsibilities, freedom without boundaries. He wanted to be God over his own life. And that is precisely our sin too. Sin is rebellion, sin is God-playing, sin is man's will exalted over and opposed to God's will. Yes, Adam is everyone.

Alas, the broken image! Earth is no longer submissive but hostile, bringing forth thorns and thistles unto man, converting his work into drudgery. The man-to-earth relationship is violated, and all our pollution of the environment is the continued story of Eden spoiled. The man-to-others relationship is also disrupted, and the story of Abel's death at the hands of Cain follows hard upon the Fall—and continues through the ages. Worst of all, the man-to-God relationship is shattered. God comes and man hides. Alienation has supplanted communion. But thank God, the story of Adam—the story of ourselves—does not end there.

III. THE REMAKING OF ADAM IS THE WORK OF CHRIST

The first promise of a Redeemer is couched in cryptic words. To the serpent-tempter God says, "I will put enmity between you and the woman, and between your seed and her seed; he shall bruise your head, and you shall bruise his heel" (3:15). The hope of the restored image was kept alive through ancient centuries by a procession of divine words and deeds that came with growing clarity.

And then Jesus came—the seed of the woman, born of the Virgin Mary to "destroy the works of the devil" (1 John 3:8). Sin bruised Him on the Cross, but He overcame sin. His death atones for sin. It judges evil. It liberates the trusting soul. It reconciles the believer to God. Communion is restored, and man becomes truly human again.

*   *   *

Made, unmade, remade. That is the story of Adam, of mankind, of you and me.

Have you received Christ? Are you living in communion with God and in peace with others? Have the broken relationships of your life been healed?

The entrance to Eden has been lost. We cannot go back to the unspoiled garden. But the way has been opened to the city of God and to the tree of life. And a voice says, "Come."

3

Where Are You?

The first question God ever put to man was brief and probing.

> *Where are you?* (Gen. 3:9).

Until Adam sinned, the question would have been pointless. God knew where man was, and man knew where he was, for they joyfully fellowshipped together.

But sin alienates. Sin destroys relationships. Sin brings estrangement, distrust, and fear to the sinner's heart. So the first reaction of sinning man and woman was their futile attempt to hide from God.

I. GOD KNEW WHERE ADAM WAS

Trees cannot hide a person from the God who sees all and knows all. When God asks, "Where are you?" He is not seeking information. Rather, He is compelling sinners to face up to their lost condition, to recognize the mess they have made of their lives. Yes, God knew where Adam was, but Adam needed to know, just as we need to know where we are in relationship to God.

The man who could not hide among the trees tried to hide behind his wife. When faced with his sin, Adam claimed to have eaten the forbidden fruit to please her. Indirectly, but not too subtly, he even tried to shift the blame to God, saying, "The woman whom *thou* gavest to be with me, she gave me fruit of the tree, and I ate" (v. 12, emphasis added). The woman, in turn, tried to pin the blame on the tempter: "The serpent beguiled me, and I ate" (v. 13).

From the reactions of Adam and Eve we can see that

II. HUMAN NATURE IS UNCHANGED SINCE THE FALL

The attempt to hide from God and to excuse our sins is going on all the time, with the same tragic consequences today as in Adam's day.

God refused the alibis of Adam and Eve, and He will not accept yours or mine. "Each of us shall give account of himself to God" (Rom. 14:12). That is true, not only in a distant future judgment but also here and now. God makes each person responsible for his own life. Placing the blame for your misdeeds on society, or your parents, or your spouse, or your friends, or your enemies, or anyone else is wasted breath. You will never find forgiveness and peace until you take the blame squarely on yourself and confess, "I have sinned."

III. "WHERE ARE YOU?" IS GOD'S QUESTION TO US, FOR ADAM IS EVERYONE

"Adam," in Hebrew, means mankind. Where are you in relationship to God? Are you walking with Him or running from Him? Do you know Him, so that you love Him? Or do you project your own sinful, guilt-laden, failure-ridden self

14

to infinity and call *that* "god"—causing you to fear and hate the idol you have created? The God revealed in Genesis 3 is the true God, not the "god" that is manufactured by anyone's rebelling, fearing, hating mind.

(1) This true God was *slandered by Satan*

The tempter insinuated that God is not good because He abridged man's freedom. Satan's philosophy is "experience everything." If God forbids something, He is cramping man's development! Be your own god, the tempter argues; you decide what is right or wrong.

(2) This true God was *rejected by man*

Man wanted to be lord over his own life, even as he was lord over the earth. He did not want to be a steward, answering to another; he wanted to be lord, answering only to himself. And so he disobeyed, he rebelled, he sinned. The same dark reason lies at the root of all your sins too.

(3) This true God, though slandered and rejected, was *merciful to sinners*

They deserved destruction, but He continued them in existence. He expelled them from the garden, placing the tree of life beyond their reach. But God does not want us to live forever in sin, guilt, and shame! He promised a coming Redeemer—the Seed of the woman who would bruise the serpent's head, who would crush the power of Satan and rescue sinners from death.

The Bible is the story of that promise, a promise repeated, clarified, enlarged, and fulfilled. "When the time had fully come, God sent forth his Son, born of woman, born under the law, to redeem those who were under the law, so that we might receive adoption as sons" (Gal. 4:4-5). "A second Adam to the fight / And to the rescue came." Jesus Christ, "the second man," "the last Adam" (1 Cor. 15:47, 45), died for our sins and redeems us to God. By confessing our sins and believing in Him, we are forgiven and restored to fellowship with God. And that fellowship is life eternal!

*   *   *

Friend, if you have not done so, it is time to accept the blame for your own sins. It is time to hush your alibis. It is time to stop trying to hide from God. It is time to give your heart to Jesus Christ. He will pardon you, renew you, and make you His own child forever.

4

Cain, the Murderer

When man is not right with God, he will not be right with others. When he rebels against God, he will rebel against his fellowman. The man-to-man relationship is always determined by the man-to-God relationship. It is no surprise that the story of Adam's fall from God should be followed by the story of Abel's death at the hands of his brother Cain.

> *Cain rose up against Abel his brother, and slew him* (Gen. 4:8, KJV).

Jealous of Abel because the Lord seemed to favor him, Cain's smoldering anger erupted into violence, and history's first murder was committed. Reading this ancient story is like standing at the source of all the rivers of human blood that have been spilled in the crimes, riots, and wars of the centuries. God said, "The voice of your brother's blood is crying to me from the ground" (v. 10). Abel's blood is a crimson spring that gushes forth, to be fed and enlarged by the countless violent deaths of history, becoming the ocean of sin, guilt, and sorrow that now deluges our world.

This brief and simple story from the past is loaded with lessons for us today. One lesson is this:

I. VIOLENCE BEGETS VIOLENCE

Cain chose violence and murder as his problem-solving device, but violence always remains a problem, not a solution. Hatred breeds hatred, anger nourishes anger, and violence produces violence. One killing leads to another—that is the history of our own times.

Before the fourth chapter of Genesis ends, a descendant of Cain is heard confessing, "I have slain a man for wounding me" (v. 23), and boasting of his resources for retaliation if anyone seeks to avenge the killing. It sounds terribly like the politics of the 20th century!

No, violence is not a solution. No solution was found for the hate, anger, and killing until One came who was murdered at Calvary, refusing to take vengeance, bearing our guilt upon His innocence, and speaking divine forgiveness to His murderers. The blood of Jesus answers the blood of Abel.

A second lesson in this ancient story is this:

II. EVERY MAN SLAIN IS A BROTHER LOST

We are all the sons of Adam, and every person killed is our brother, whatever his race, class, or nation.

In our jealousy, hatred, and anger we try to justify our crimes by restricting the definition of brother. The Bible unites us at the beginning and thus destroys our rationale for murder. The victim is never simply "the enemy"; always the victim is "Abel your brother" (v. 9). We are made from one blood, and we have one original Father. To kill any man is to lose a brother.

A third lesson is this:

III. GOD HOLDS US ACCOUNTABLE FOR OUR BROTHERS

There is not a wasted word in the ancient record. The murder is recited, and the very next sentence reads, "Then the Lord said to Cain, 'Where is Abel your brother?'" (v. 9).

Cain lied and tried to bolster his lie with a disclaimer of responsibility. "I do not know," he responded; "am I my brother's keeper?" The answer is yes. God calls us to account for our brothers.

Accountability means punishment when the brother has been slain. The earth that received the blood of Abel becomes hostile to Cain. The slayer becomes a vagabond, viewed with distrust by society, and living in fear of an avenger. Saddest of all the statements of judgment in the story are these simple words, "Then Cain went away from the presence of the Lord" (v. 16).

Nothing relieves the tragedy of Cain but the victory of the Cross. The blood of Jesus "speaks more graciously than the blood of Abel" (Heb. 12:24). Abel's blood speaks of guilt; Jesus' blood speaks of atonement. Abel's blood cries out for justice; Jesus' blood provides mercy and forgiveness. Abel's blood voices the anguished futility of sin; Jesus' blood declares the accomplished remedy of grace. The blood of Christ can bring about the forgiveness of sins, the destruction of hatred, and the restoration of brother to brother.

* * *

God's first questions are still His questions to us today. "Where are you?" "Where is your brother?" Are you rightly related to God and to your brother? Do you have peace with God and with your brother? This righteousness and peace are possible, thanks to the blood of Jesus shed for us!

5

Where Is Your Brother?

God confronted the first murderer in the human family with a piercing question:

> *Where is Abel your brother?* (Gen. 4:9).

Cain lied, replying, "I do not know; am I my brother's keeper?" Provoked by jealousy, Cain had planned and executed the murder of Abel in cold blood.

God's first question was addressed to Adam—"Where are you?" His second question is put to Adam's son—"Where is your brother?" Adam alibied his sin, trying to shift the blame to his wife. Cain lied, angrily and blatantly. It is never far from an alibi to a lie. We begin by excusing our sins, and soon we are denying them.

The excuse and the lie were futile, for

I. NOTHING IS HIDDEN FROM GOD

God knew where Adam was. And God knew where Abel was. There is always one witness to every crime, and He knows where all the bodies are buried. Lawmen cannot find Jimmy Hoffa, but God knows who killed him and where the body was dumped. There is no escape from divine justice, whatever the limitations and failures of human justice. No man gets away with crime; the first killer did not, and the last killer will not. All the chickens come home to roost sooner or later. You cannot sin and get off scot-free.

"The wages of sin is death" (Rom. 6:23), however long pay-day is deferred.

Crime begets crime. Violence breeds violence. Sin produces a chain reaction. Jack Finegan refers to Cain's act as "Murder Inaugurated." The earth has become so full of violence, the human heart so full of hatred, that plenty of killers can now be hired. From "Murder Inaugurated" we have come to "Murder Incorporated." Evil is the fastest-growing and farthest-spreading of all contagions.

Adam's disobedience could not be contained; it spilled over into his family. Cain's murder could not be isolated; it became a rapid, widening stream. By chapter 6 of this ancient volume God is heard saying, "The earth is filled with violence" (v. 13). We cannot control sin. Like a forest fire in high winds, it rages out of control, spreading destruction everywhere.

While we cannot control sin, we are responsible for it.

II. GOD HOLDS US ACCOUNTABLE FOR OTHERS

"Where is your brother?" Life is not a game of solitaire. To be human is to live in relationships, and these relationships expand and intensify responsibility. Cain tried in vain to repudiate this responsibility, snapping insolently at God, "Am I my brother's keeper?" But God brushed aside his snarling disclaimer and pressed home his guilt: "What have you done? The voice of your brother's blood is crying to me from the ground" (v. 10).

We are "keepers" of our brothers, or we are rebels against God. The strong should support the weak, the wealthy should serve the needy, and those who have found favor with God should seek the lost. We cannot blame others for our sins, but we cannot exclude them from our lives. We must answer to God for ourselves and for others.

21

"Where are you?" "Where is your brother?" The two questions are inextricably linked.

Guilt spawns fear. Cain was afraid that he would be hated, feared, and killed by someone pretending to avenge Abel. Then he learned a great lesson:

III. GOD'S RIGHTEOUS JUDGMENT IS TEMPERED WITH MERCY

"The Lord put a mark on Cain, lest any who came upon him should kill him" (v. 15). What that "mark" was we do not know—perhaps some "visible and indelible mark of infamy and disgrace." But it was also a reminder of divine mercy. The Lord continues the killer in existence, not to condone his crime, but to create time and space for repentance. Unless he repented, judgment without mercy finally had to come, for God cannot ignore sin. His justice must be served, otherwise His holiness would be tainted.

As a consequence of his sin Cain became "a fugitive and a wanderer on the earth" (vv. 12, 14). The earth that drinks the victim's blood can never be the sinner's home. Sin creates a restlessness, a homelessness that can only be satisfied with a pardon from God and a welcome into heaven. This world is too filled with sin and death to fulfill the homing instinct of the human race. Like Cain, we all wander "east of Eden" until we reach "the better country."

God said, "The voice of your brother's blood is crying to me from the ground." The New Testament declares that the blood of Jesus "speaks more graciously than the blood of Abel" (Heb. 12:24). Abel's blood cried out for wrong to be righted, for sin to be remedied. The human economy could *avenge* blood with blood. The divine economy *atones* for blood with blood. Through the blood of Christ every sinner who repents and believes can be forgiven, restored, and brought home to God.

To deny sin is to avert mercy. To confess and forsake sin is to receive mercy (see Prov. 28:13). The man in our Lord's parable of justification prayed as we all should do—"God, be merciful to me a sinner!" (Luke 18:13).

*   *   *

Is that your prayer? If that is your heart's sincere cry, here is the Lord's gracious response: "Your sins are forgiven."

6

Walk with God

In simple words the Bible sums up the life of a rare man.

> *Enoch walked with God; and he was not, for God took him* (Gen. 5:24).

These words flash like a jewel set in an otherwise dreary wall. Genesis 5 contains a genealogy, and genealogies are not exciting to read. "All scripture is inspired" (2 Tim. 3:16), but not all Scripture is inspiring. Here a dusty catalog of names—of births, numbers, and deaths—is suddenly interrupted to pay tribute to a most unusual man. "Enoch walked with God." While others were dancing with the devil, this man walked with God. He became thereby a challenge to us all.

I. Enoch's decision challenges us

"Enoch walked with God," we are told, "after the birth of Methuselah" (v. 22). Did the child's birth evoke the father's decision? The Bible doesn't say, but I cannot think of a better reason to walk with God.

The responsibility of rearing children ought to bring a man or woman to God. Providing and guiding as a father demands wisdom, patience, and strength that only God can supply. Pressures and trials of parenthood, in a world filled with rebellion, grief, and pain, produce sorrow only God can comfort. All men need God, but the man who is raising sons and daughters, who is sharing the burdens of marriage and family, doubly needs to walk with God.

If you do not walk with God, can you expect your children to serve Him? A father who walks with God is not guaranteed that his children will. But if he does not, chances that they never will are multiplied. Dad, if your youngsters duplicate your private character and public life, will they know God and reach heaven? Where are your footsteps leading them?

II. ENOCH'S DIRECTION CHALLENGES US

"Enoch walked with God"; he took God's direction. God is utterly sovereign. He knows where He is going, and He knows where we should be going. He does not allow us to fix the direction or to set the pace. The Psalmist declared, "The steps of a man are from the Lord, and he establishes him in whose way he delights; though he fall, he shall not be cast headlong, for the Lord is the stay of his hand" (37:23-24). When you keep step with God, you will not find the road always smooth, but you will find pleasure and protection as the Heavenly Father holds the hand of His faltering child.

If we insist on choosing the direction, we must walk without God. We will then condemn ourselves to mill around in the wastelands of sin, guilt, despair, frustration, and emptiness. When God came in Jesus Christ, He said to men, "Follow me." He did not consent to walk with them in paths of their own choosing. Rather, He called them to forsake their ways, ways strewn with human wrecks, and to walk in His way. The prophet Jeremiah exclaimed, "I know, O Lord, that the way of man is not in himself, that it is not in man who walks to direct his steps" (10:23). When man charts the course, he heads straight for hell. True life, eternal life, can be found only when God says, "This is the way, walk in it" (Isa. 30:21).

III. ENOCH'S DESTINY CHALLENGES US

"Enoch walked with God" and "God took him." What a glorious destination! He went to God's house. Someone said, "Enoch went to spend the night with God, and he is still in heaven, for there is no night there."

The New Testament interprets the words, "he was not, for God took him." Heb. 11:5 tells us, "By faith Enoch was taken up so that he should not see death; and he was not found, because God had taken him. Now before he was taken he was attested as having pleased God."

God does not spare from death all who walk with Him. But when the path He chooses for us passes through the dark gates of death, He shares that path with us. He will not forsake us when we are dying. As the apostle Paul affirmed, death cannot "separate us from the love of God in Christ Jesus our Lord" (Rom. 8:38-39).

Enoch's earthly life was short when measured against others of that day. He serves to remind us that quality of life means more than quantity of life. *How* is more important than *how long.* When a man walks with God, he will live forever. How much of his life is spent on earth is insignificant.

26

You can be gone from earth sooner than you expect. As Thomas Fuller said, "Death keeps no calendar." People die at all ages. What matters is their destination, not the length of the road. If you walk with God, your destination is heaven, a perfect society, unmarred by sin, pain, death, or grief.

*   *   *

A Chinese proverb says, "To know the road ahead, ask those coming back." No one comes back on this road. Only God can guide you home. Walk with Him!

7

A Man Who Saved His Family

*Noah was a righteous man, blameless in his
generation; Noah walked with God* (Gen. 6:9).

Enoch walked with God, and God took him to heaven.
Noah walked with God, and God left him on earth. God
does not treat all His people alike, but He treats them all
justly. That is a difficult lesson for us to learn, but our peace
of mind depends on learning it. We can go through hard
places whining, "Why me?" or we can go through them saying, "Why not me?" Noah was a man of intrepid faith, and
we can learn valuable lessons from him. Let's look at some
of them.

I. NOAH LIVED A GOOD LIFE IN EVIL TIMES

In his day the earth had become so wicked and filled
with violence that God was "grieved." In the quaint words
of Gen. 6:6, "The Lord was sorry that he had made man on
the earth."

In that mass of corruption one man stood out like a
diamond on a garbage heap. "Noah was a righteous man,
blameless in his generation; Noah walked with God." Mor-
ally and spiritually Noah towered over his contemporaries, a
colossus among pygmies. He is abiding proof that we do not
have to be shaped and determined by the evil factors in our

heredity and environment. The example of Noah makes a liar out of every person who pleads the influence of his surroundings as an excuse for his sins.

By the grace of God a man or a woman can live the best of lives in the worst of times. We can walk with God when all around us people are running with the devil. As the apostle Paul put it, "Where sin increased, grace abounded all the more" (Rom. 5:20). It is grace and choice, not heritage and environment, that makes the man.

II. Noah Saved His Family When the World Was Lost

The invitation of God, issued a week before the rains began and the Flood came, included Noah's family. "Go into the ark, you and all your household, for I have seen that you are righteous before me in this generation" (Gen. 7:1). In the words of the New Testament, "By faith Noah, being warned by God concerning events as yet unseen, took heed and constructed an ark for the saving of his household" (Heb. 11:7).

Like Noah, we have been warned by God of a coming judgment. In the Bible, God has testified against the sins of our desperately evil and violent society. Upon those sins His wrath will be outpoured. As the world ripens for judgment and hastens to its doom, a man's first concern should be the salvation of his family.

God has prepared an ark in which all who believe may be saved. In the life, death, and resurrection of Jesus Christ, God has acted mightily and graciously to provide deliverance from sin and wrath. This saving Christ can be your Christ and the Christ of your family. As Paul said to the jailer at Philippi, "Believe in the Lord Jesus and you will be saved, you and your household" (Acts 16:31).

Fathers, listen to the Word of God. Evil forces abound that menace your homes. The world, in its moral corruption, threatens to ruin forever your marriage and your family. Like Noah, you are responsible for living a good life in evil times. You are responsible for supplying your family with the example of a man who will stand against the raging tides of unbelief and immorality, who will stand for God and truth and right whatever the cost. If your life, your faith, your prayers, your moral commitment will not direct your family's minds toward God, what will? You cannot shift the heavy responsibility for righteous influence to another. You must stand in the midst of evil and say, as did old Joshua, "But as for me and my house, we will serve the Lord" (Josh. 24:15). The finest legacy any man can bequeath to his children is not money or property but the testimony of a godly faith.

When the world perished, Noah saved his family. They joined him in the ark, convinced that he was right and the world was wrong. What a tribute their presence in the ark was to Noah's love, faith, prayers, and example—and to God's infinite mercy in the midst of wrath.

*   *   *

Are you living for God in a godless age? Are you in the ark? Is your family in the ark? Judgment is coming. Though the world scoffs, though sin abounds, judgment is coming! But Jesus Christ can save you from sin and prepare you for judgment. In His love He extends to you an invitation: "Go into the ark, you and all your household."

8

The Ark or the Flood

Even folks who never read the Bible know about Noah and the ark and the Flood. It is difficult, however, for anyone to appreciate the struggle that must have occurred in Noah's heart when

The Lord said . . . , "Go into the ark" (Gen. 7:1).

"Lord," he may have asked, "is there no other way to be saved? I built this boat by Your plans, and I am sure it will float—but all these animals, and this whole family, including daughters-in-law, shut up together for who knows how long!"

Perhaps the Lord responded, "It is the ark or the Flood, Noah. Those are your only choices. Now get in the boat and do not argue. Take it a day at a time, and you will be all right."

So in he went, and soon began

I. A RUGGED CRUISE

It was worse than Noah expected. Imagine rain drumming on the roof incessantly for 40 days and nights! Imagine the endless squawking, squealing, braying, whickering, growling, bleating, lowing, cooing, cawing, whistling, chirping, and roaring of animals and birds! Imagine the creaking of timbers and lapping of waves, and through it all the strain on nerves of living cooped up with people, each of whom was different from the others!

The ark was a primitive tub, not the *Queen Elizabeth II* by any stretch of the imagination. There were no showers, no toilets, no deodorants. No elegant cuisine tickled the palate, no programmed entertainment broke the monotony, no air-conditioning relieved the muggy heat. No, the ark was a floating zoo—cramped, crowded, and comfortless. The stench of manure, of sweat, of unwashed bodies, of piled-up trash must have been awful. And there was not even a Gideon Bible to read for comfort!

How frayed the nerves of people and animals must have become! They were in that ark for over a year.

I can imagine Shem's wife saying, "I am sick of this bobbing tub! Sick of these grunting, growling beasts! Sick of these chattering birds! Sick of the stink and racket and darkness! If I don't see the sun and feel the earth soon, I will go mad! Do something!"

And maybe Shem replied, "So, go back to your mother."

I can imagine Ham's wife screaming, "I quit! I quit! I didn't marry you to slop hogs and chase camels. I have had it with balky goats and bird droppings and in-laws. I am through!"

And maybe Ham yelled back, "Would you rather swim?"

I can imagine Japheth saying, "You know, Dad, when you started talking rain and building this ark, I thought you were slightly unhinged. When drunks laughed and neighbors mocked, I was embarrassed. I even thought of leaving home. But I am glad you really did know the difference between God's voice and noises in the head. For all the work and stench and monotony, it is good to be here and not out there where life has disappeared."

And maybe Noah smiled and said, "Yes, Son, the ark is an awkward-looking thing, and it is smelly and cramped and nerve-racking. The days are long, the work is hard, and the crew gets depressed at times. Still, it is a grand old boat, lad, for it is saving our family. When things are at their worst, I just say to myself, 'Old man, it sure beats drowning.'"

Does any of this have meaning for us? Yes, it bears to us

II. A SERIOUS LESSON

The Church is like the ark—something for the world to scorn, but God's way of saving His people from the coming judgment upon sin. God is not saving us as individuals merely. He is saving a family. Salvation is personal, but it is not private.

And believe me, the Church is far from perfect and not always pleasant. There are some strange beasts—clean and unclean—in the Church. And there is hard work to do, irritating conditions to endure, and exasperating persons to accept. To the world it is a joke, to itself it is a trial, but it certainly beats the alternative.

A judgment is coming upon the world, a judgment worse than the ancient Flood. Peter describes it in these words: "The heavens will pass away with a loud noise, and the elements will be dissolved with fire, and the earth and the works that are upon it will be burned up" (2 Pet. 3:10). The fire next time! When that comes, the Church will be saved, to inhabit "new heavens and a new earth in which righteousness dwells" (v. 13).

The ark or the Flood! The Church or the fire! Perhaps the sweetest words Noah ever heard were those spoken by God when the waters of the Flood had abated: "Go forth from the ark" (Gen. 8:16). But while rain was falling, waters were rising, and life was vanishing, Noah would say, "The ark beats the Flood."

*   *   *

Come into the ark! It is your only hope!

9

The Bow and the Babe

After the Flood, when Noah left the ark, "God put a rainbow in the sky." He said,

I set my bow in the cloud, and it shall be a sign of the covenant between me and the earth (Gen. 9:13).

Each time a rainbow appears, it proclaims the covenant promise of God: "The waters shall never again become a flood to destroy all flesh" (v. 15).

God keeps His word. Throughout the centuries local floods have devastated limited areas, but universal deluge and destruction have not occurred. Sinful, rebellious, undeserving mankind has been continued in existence. God has given us time, space, incentive, and freedom to repent of our sins and to seek His forgiveness.

The rainbow is a beautiful sign of a gracious covenant. A rainbow splashed against a storm cloud is one of the most cheering sights in the world. But God has given us

I. A LOVELIER SIGN, A BETTER COVENANT

At every Advent season we celebrate this lovelier sign, this better covenant. When Jesus was born in Bethlehem, an angel appeared to certain shepherds who were "keeping watch over their flock by night" (Luke 2:8). To those startled shepherds the angel of God delivered history's most significant birth announcement: "To you is born this day in the city of David a Savior, who is Christ the Lord. And this will be a sign for you: you will find a babe wrapped in swaddling cloths and lying in a manger" (vv. 11-12).

The shepherds hurried to Bethlehem "and found Mary and Joseph, and the babe lying in a manger" (v. 16). The Savior of the world was resting on a bed of straw!

Nobody hears a rainbow. Suddenly it is there, and we catch sight of it and thrill to it, and those who know the Bible rejoice in its meaning. Trumpets did not sound when Christ was born. Proud hands did not lift Him from a palace balcony for admiring throngs to cheer. There was no dancing in the streets, no parties in the pubs, no strutting headlines or billboards across the land. A quiet young woman, denied a room at the crowded inn, delivered her Child in a cattle stall. But that Child was the Word of God become flesh. The Creator became a creature, eternity invaded history, all without fanfare and ballyhoo.

The silent rainbow declares that God will spare the earth from destruction by flood. The Babe in the manger declares that God will save sinners from damnation. God has solemnly promised to save from sin and bring to heaven all who trust in Jesus Christ. His peace and goodwill toward men smiled at adoring shepherds from a crib of straw. What an incomparable sign! What a gracious covenant!

Comparing the Babe to the bow, we have also

II. A COSTLIER COVENANT, A GREATER SALVATION

The God who set a bow in the clouds planted a cross in the ground. The Babe who was laid in the manger became the Man who was hung on the Cross. There "Christ died for our sins in accordance with the scriptures" (1 Cor. 15:3). He gave himself, by the will of God, for the salvation of mankind. His wounding was for our healing. His death was for our life.

The rainbow pledges protection against a global flood. It does not secure against nuclear holocaust—or any other destruction mankind may bring upon itself. But Jesus Christ secures us against anything and everything that seeks to destroy our souls. Listen to the confidence inspired by the cross of Christ in a believer's heart: "I am sure that neither death, nor life, nor angels, nor principalities, nor things present, nor things to come, nor powers, nor height, nor depth, nor anything else in all creation, will be able to separate us from the love of God in Christ Jesus our Lord" (Rom. 8:38-39).

The bow in the cloud was the token of "the . . . covenant between God and every living creature" (Gen. 9:16). And the Babe in the manger was God's sign "to all the people" (Luke 2:10). When the Babe became the Man, and the manger led to the Cross, His atoning death was for all the world. "For God so loved the world that he gave his only Son, that whoever believes in him should not perish but have eternal life" (John 3:16). "And he is the atoning sacrifice . . . for the sins of the whole world" (1 John 2:2, NRSV). God's provision to save cannot include everyone without including you and me!

* * *

As did the ancient shepherds, let us come with haste to Jesus Christ, confessing Him as our Savior and Lord today. He is God's rainbow of grace athwart the storm clouds of sin and death.

Wordsworth exclaimed, "My heart leaps up when I behold / A rainbow in the sky." How much more when we behold the Christ of God!

10

The March of Faith

God needed a pioneer. He wanted someone to launch a new movement in history, a movement that would continue for centuries, a movement that would shape events and people for time and eternity. This movement, this history within history, would involve nations and kings and would run the gamut of human experience—birth and death, slavery and freedom, war and peace, faith and apostasy, hope and despair, love and hate. This movement, in the fullness of time, would thrust into the hands of mankind the Bible and would produce for mankind the Savior.

But that movement had to start somewhere with someone. God needed a pioneer, a man of courage, vision, and—above all—faith. Here is the simply worded account of the launching of that movement, a quiet trickle that will become a great ocean:

> *Now the Lord said to Abram, "Go from your country and your kindred and your father's house to the land that I will show you. And I will make of you a great nation, and I will bless you, and make your name*

*great, so that you will be a blessing. I will bless
those who bless you, and him who curses you I will
curse; and in you all the families of the earth shall
be blessed"* [margin]. *So Abram went, as the Lord
had told him* (Gen. 12:1-4).

Yes, God needed a path-breaker, so

I. GOD CREATED A PIONEER

Why Abram? The question tantalizes, for we know almost nothing about him prior to this call to pioneer God's
movement. That is just the point! Abram was not qualified
for this adventure of faith by nature, or by heredity, or by
environment. God was not choosing between candidates,
screening them through psychological or aptitude tests in
order to find His man. When God wanted a pioneer, He
created that pioneer. The calling was the creating. The word
God spoke to Abram was a self-authenticating, self-fulfill-
ing word. It contained within itself the power to awaken
response, the power to make Abram a man of faith—obedient, daring, persistent faith.

Measured by any human criteria for greatness, Abram
became a great man. But in the beginning he was nobody,
and the only greatness that appears is God's—the greatness
of love, mercy, and wisdom that resolved to provide rescue
from sin and death for a world gone haywire in its revolt
against Him. The power that initiates this movement is not
human but divine. Hear God speaking: "I will show you . . .
I will make of you . . . I will bless you." This covenant does
not rest upon the fickle, fragile resolution of man, but on the
immutable, invincible will of God Almighty.

What God plans to do, evil men will seek to prevent
and destroy. Blood will flow, warriors will scream, women
will sob, slaves will groan, and graves will multiply as

through the centuries wicked and misguided men oppose the covenant with Abram. But no one and no thing can stop God from fulfilling His purpose. Before He is through, one grave will be emptied. A crucified Messiah will rise again with power to save forever all who believe in Him. In Jesus Christ, slain for our transgressions and raised from the dead for our justification, God's promise to bless all nations of earth through Abram will be fulfilled.

The pioneer could not know that all this would happen, but at the word of God

II. ABRAM BEGAN THE MARCH OF FAITH

"He went out, not knowing where he was to go" (Heb. 11:8). For the sake of the covenant, for the sake of the coming Christ, Abram forsook his native land, his ancestral home, his supportive kinsmen, and risked the unknown. A "better country" awaited him (v. 16). A lasting city beckoned him onward. And a numberless family will share that eternal inheritance with him—the redeemed of all ages and nations, the believing children of believing Abram.

That march of faith would end only at death. In this world Abram never realized the promise. He only glimpsed it afar off. Through thick and thin, through joy and sorrow, he persevered, convinced beyond anyone's counterarguments that the God who promised was faithful. He lived his whole life through as a pilgrim whose homeland was still beyond his farthest footsteps.

III. WE ARE CALLED TO JOIN THAT PILGRIMAGE TO HEAVEN

We are summoned to believe in Jesus Christ and thus become children of the pioneer Abram. Like him, we must be willing to obey God's call, even if it means severing every earthly tie, risking every familiar support, and enduring every possible outrage. Jesus Christ says, "Follow me." He gives no road map. He promises no easy trail. He guarantees no popular support. He speaks instead of crosses, of persecutions, of temptations, and of service that will drain the last drop of your blood for the sake of others.

Do we tremble in hesitation, knowing our weakness, recalling our failures, fearing the unknown? We must not look at ourselves. We must not ask for assurances. We make this journey, "looking to Jesus the pioneer and perfecter of our faith" (Heb. 12:2). He goes with us, saying, "I will never fail you nor forsake you" (13:5). That is enough!

* * *

I challenge you today! Believe God. Venture at His word. Press forward into His new life of forgiveness, peace, and joy. You cannot know all that will happen, but you will find beneath your marching feet the everlasting granite of His unshakable promises!

Jesus Christ, the Son of Abraham, is the world's only Savior. He alone can lead you to the promised land of endless and boundless fulfillment. Put your trust in Him, and set your feet in His footsteps. You will never regret the march of faith.

11

The Man of Faith

When God said, "Go," Abraham went. He had no road map, and he asked no sign. He trusted God to fulfill the promise, "I will show you." At the age of 75 he hit the trail as a pioneer, a man of faith.

His faith was not perfect. When famine struck the land of Canaan, Abraham sought refuge in Egypt. There, to insure his own life, he passed off his wife as his sister. It was a half-truth, but "half-truths become whole lies." The ruse backfired, and Abraham was ordered to leave.

But if his faith was not perfect, it was persistent. The dominant feature of his life was not wealth, though he was "very rich" (Gen. 13:2). Nor was it courage, though he could muster a small army and do battle with kings to rescue his nephew Lot, who had been taken prisoner (14:14-24). Neither was it his prayers, though he stood tall as an intercessor before the Lord (18:17-33). No, the outstanding feature of Abraham's life was his faith. He is the father of all who are justified by faith, the first of whom it was said,

> *He believed the Lord; and he reckoned it to him as righteousness* (15:6).

Let us examine Abraham's faith for the sake of our own.

I. ABRAHAM BELIEVED IN THE LORD'S PROMISE

The Lord said to him, "I will make of you a great nation, and I will bless you, and make your name great, so that you will be a blessing. I will bless those who bless you, and him who curses you I will curse; and in you all the families of the earth shall be blessed" (12:2-3, margin).

When the fulfillment of that promise seemed to be humanly impossible, Abraham clung to it in passionate trust. And he trusted in the word of God without the support of any signs. It was enough for him that God had spoken. The word of the Lord was the whole ground of his confidence. In his old age, therefore, he could laugh with joy at the prospect of a child with whom the covenant would be established. Sarah laughed, too, but in the bitterness of doubt (see 18:12-15). Abraham seems to have laughed in the exuberance of faith (17:15-17).

The promise of God alone is the ground of faith.

II. ABRAHAM BELIEVED IN THE LORD'S POWER

Read the opening verses of Genesis 12, where the covenant promises of God are first recorded. Over and over occur the words, "I will . . ." "I will show you." "I will make of you a great nation." "I will bless you, and make your name great." "I will bless those who bless you." In later conversations with Abraham the Lord repeats this solemn "I will" dozens of times. Emphasis remains throughout on the weakness of Abraham and the sovereign power of God. His challenge abides: "Is anything too hard for the Lord?" (18:14).

Centuries later, when the Lord's covenant with Abraham had been fulfilled, Scripture would say of that gallant pioneer of faith, "No distrust made him waver concerning the promise of God, but he grew strong in his faith as he gave glory to God, fully convinced that God was able to do what he had promised" (Rom. 4:20-21). God is able to perform His promises! That was Abraham's abiding confidence.

If faith is weak, it has been reposed in failing man, not in the invincible God.

III. ABRAHAM BELIEVED IN THE LORD'S PURPOSES

Through the seed of Abraham "all the families of the earth" were to "be blessed." One man was chosen. From that one man's loins would come nations. One of those nations would give to the world the Bible and the Christ, and thus the blessing of Abraham would come upon the whole world.

God "tested" Abraham. He called upon him to offer Isaac, the heir of the covenant, as a sacrifice. Abraham obeyed, and only the Lord's last-minute intervention prevented him from slaying his son upon an altar. Abraham was sure that God's purposes could not fail, not even if the fulfillment of those purposes required the resurrection of Isaac from the dead (Genesis 22; Heb. 11:17-19).

What God is doing provides mankind with its only hope of deliverance from sin and death. His purposes cannot be defeated!

* * *

What has all of this to say to us? Well, God has kindly thrust His Word into our hands. The Bible records the fulfillment of the covenant with Abraham. It extends to us promises of salvation from sin through Jesus Christ. It adds to those the gracious promises of God's keeping power and the promises of a "better country" where sin, sorrow, and suffering are banished forever. It calls upon us, like the patriarch of old, to live by faith.

44

Abraham is a witness to us that God can be trusted. I ask you, then, are you trusting His Word and power today? Have you included yourself, by faith, in His saving purposes? Are you a child of Abraham, bound for glory? Faith brings life, unbelief brings death. The choice is yours.

12

Ancient City, Modern Sin

Beneath the salt-heavy waters of the Dead Sea lie the ruins of ancient Sodom. The city perished under the wrath of God. Fire and brimstone fell from heaven as a judgment upon the sexual perversion that raged like an epidemic in that concentration of corruption. In simple words that would terrify our modern cities, were they not so case-hardened against moral truth, that judgment is recorded:

God destroyed the cities of the valley (Gen. 19:29).

In this portion of Holy Writ we are introduced to

I. AN AWFUL SIN

Sodom has given its name to a revolting practice—homosexual behavior. Sodomy is everywhere condemned in the Bible. The face of God is set against this evil, and He will judge it in His righteous wrath. Sodomy has been a moral blight upon a fallen race throughout history, but never has it been more rampant than today. And never has it been so brash and arrogant, demanding approval as an acceptable "alternative" life-style. It has invaded halls of learning, courts of justice, and pulpits of churches. But though 10,000 prophets of Baal plead for it, sodomy is stamped as evil and marked for judgment by the holy God.

"God remembered Abraham, and sent Lot out of the midst of the overthrow" (v. 29). The intercession of Abraham, "the friend of God," is recorded in Genesis 18. Abraham prayed for Lot, but he did not plead for sodomy. He knew how God felt about homosexual behavior, and he did not attempt to call darkness light. More wicked than the ancient Sodomites are the modern ministers who, knowing the plain teaching of the Bible, have become defenders and advocates of evil.

The awful sin provoked

II. A TERRIBLE DOOM

God destroyed those centers of bestiality in His holy anger.

In a sense, and to a measure, God's wrath already abides upon those who practice sodomy. Diseases that are devastating to bodies and minds are epidemic within the miscalled "gay" communities. The chilling words of Romans 1 are terribly relevant to our society:

> *God gave them up in the lusts of their hearts to impurity, to the dishonoring of their bodies among themselves, because they exchanged the truth about God for a lie and worshiped and served the creature rather than the Creator, who is blessed for ever! Amen. For this reason God gave them up to dishonorable passions. Their women exchanged natural relations for unnatural, and the men likewise gave up natural relations with women and were consumed with passion for one another, men*

> *committing shameless acts with men and receiving*
> *in their own persons the due penalty for their error*
> (vv. 24-27).

When the creature becomes his own god, rejecting and defying the moral laws of the Creator, he reaps in his own flesh the judgment suited to his sin.

Homosexual behavior is but one sin among many that, according to Romans 1, provokes the wrath of God and deserves death. The entire list, drawn up as an indictment against the ancient world, is being duplicated daily in our time. God has not changed His mind about sin, and dire warnings of coming judgment are found throughout His Word. The day is coming when He will bring down the curtain on history, and that judgment will make the destruction of two ancient cities seem like a minor incident by comparison.

> *The day of the Lord will come like a thief, and then*
> *the heavens will pass away with a loud noise, and*
> *the elements will be dissolved with fire, and the*
> *earth and the works that are upon it will be burned*
> *up* (2 Pet. 3:10).

Between God's promise of judgment upon Sodom and the holocaust that destroyed that city only a day passed. Twenty centuries have elapsed since the warning of a greater and final overthrow of earth was issued as the Word of God. Nevertheless, God keeps His Word, and that terrible judgment is surely coming.

From that awesome coming wrath there is

III. A GRACIOUS ESCAPE

Before Sodom's doom occurred, God remembered Abraham and delivered Lot. Through the intercession of a greater than Abraham, pardoned sinners will escape the coming ultimate judgment. That intercession is recorded in one of the richest affirmations of mercy to be found within the Bible: "He is able for all time to save those who draw near to God through him, since he always lives to make intercession for them" (Heb. 7:25).

Jesus Christ, the Mediator, is the only hope of sodomites and all other sinners. He saves from sin and shelters from wrath all who repent of their sins and believe in His words. Judgment is coming as sure as God is holy and true. For every person, without exception, it will be Christ or endless destruction. The words of an old song probe our hearts: "Are you ready for that day to come?"

Jesus said, "Unless you repent you will . . . perish" (Luke 13:3, 5). We must turn from our sins or perish in our sins. We must put our trust in Christ or suffer the wrath of God. There is no other way of escape. There is no other means of salvation. The stupid bravado that sneers at the gospel and flaunts its ongoing sin will turn to sheer dismay in the day of judgment. Any fool can laugh his way to hell, but no one ever laughed his way out of hell.

*　*　*

God is not trifling with sin. God is not issuing idle threats. God is not making empty promises. It's time to get serious about sin and salvation. It is time to seek the Lord!

13

Where Is the Lamb?

One of the most poignant stories ever told is found in Genesis 22. To Abraham, when he was 100 years old, God had given a son. Through that son, Isaac, the divine promise of descendants—including the nation of Israel and the Savior of the world—would be fulfilled. And now "God tested Abraham" by commanding him to offer Isaac as a sacrifice upon Mount Moriah.

Father and son climbed the mountain in silence. The pain in Abraham's heart must have numbed his lips. His faith triumphed over his anguish, however. If God had made promises that must be fulfilled through Isaac, then God would keep His word if it required the raising of Isaac from the dead. To the servants who had shared the three-day journey to the base of the mountain, Abraham had said, "Stay here . . . I and the lad will go yonder and worship, and come again to you" (v. 5). I *and the lad* will come again!

On the mountain trail Isaac broke the silence with a question that must have stabbed the heart of Abraham more deeply than a knife could pierce the chest of Isaac:

> *My father! . . . Behold, the fire and the wood; but where is the lamb for a burnt offering?* (v. 7).

With a wisdom greater than he knew, Abraham replied, "God will provide himself the lamb" (v. 8).

We encounter in this story

I. MAN'S ANGUISHED QUESTION: "WHERE IS THE LAMB?"

Most of us are familiar with the story's happy ending. Isaac was bound and laid on the altar. The knife was raised, poised for the fatal stroke. But God stayed the hand of obedient, trusting Abraham, directing him to a substitute offering—"a ram caught in a thicket by his horns" (v. 13). The grateful patriarch offered up the ram "instead of his son."

"Where is the lamb?" That is the question wrung from the anguished heart of sinful men during long centuries. Where is the sacrifice for sin? Where is the substitute whose death can reconcile guilty man to holy God? Where is the provision for our forgiveness, the forgiveness necessary to peace and fellowship with God? That question would not be finally answered until Jesus came. He was and is

II. GOD'S GRACIOUS ANSWER: "BEHOLD THE LAMB!"

Into the history of the covenant people, from the womb of a descendant of faithful Abraham, came Jesus Christ. And a rugged prophet named John, whose mission was to introduce the Messiah, looked upon Jesus and exclaimed, "Behold, the Lamb of God, who takes away the sin of the world!" (John 1:29; see 36).

Abraham's son was spared, for Isaac, as dear as he was to his father's heart, could not atone for sin. Like other men, including the giants of faith, Isaac had sinned and come short of the the glory of God. Only the sinless One could atone for the sinful many. Only an unblemished lamb could be offered to God as a sacrifice. And so it was necessary for

51

God to provide himself a Lamb, to send His Son into the world as a man among men, and to send Him to the Cross as a substitute for sinners.

> When the time had fully come, God sent forth his Son, born of woman, born under the law, to redeem those who were under the law, so that we might receive adoption as sons (Gal. 4:4-5).

Isaac was spared, but God "did not spare his own Son but gave him up for us all" (Rom. 8:32).

God did not spare His own Son, but He did raise Him from the dead! Risen from the dead, and alive forever, Jesus Christ has power to save from sin and from death all who believe in Him. For His sake God forgives our sins. By His Spirit God renews our lives. We are pardoned, who had rebelled against God. We are reconciled, who had been alienated from God. We are reborn, who had been dead in sins. We are adopted, who had been orphaned by sin. By the grace of God, beyond the comprehension of our minds and the descriptive power of our words, we are redeemed "with the precious blood of Christ, like that of a lamb without blemish or spot" (1 Pet. 1:19).

"Behold the Lamb!" We are saved by simply "looking to Jesus." In looking to Him, we look away from ourselves, we look away from each other, we look away from all human achievements, all human failures, for none of these can save us. God has provided a Lamb! To look to any other is to rebel against God and add to our sins. To look to Him is to find pardon and peace, to find life and joy.

*   *   *

"Where is the lamb?" He is right here, closer to you than the blood in your veins, closer than the breath in your lungs. He has

drawn near to offer you His salvation today. He offers it upon terms that the weakest and vilest can meet: "Behold, the Lamb of God, who takes away the sin of the world!" Behold! Simply look to Him in faith, bringing nothing to Him but your broken, empty heart. In sheer love for you, He will take away your sins and give you peace.

14

The Profane Man

In very simple words a great personal tragedy can be recorded. Of one such tragedy we read:

Thus Esau despised his birthright (Gen. 25:34).

In the New Testament, Esau is called an "irreligious" or "profane" (KJV) man (Heb. 12:16). He valued the material more than the spiritual. He was sensual and secular, and there are millions like him in our world today. Indeed, who of us is not tempted to repeat his folly?

I. ESAU VALUED HIS STOMACH ABOVE HIS SOUL

He came in from the fields one day "famished" (Gen. 25:29). His brother Jacob had cooked a savory stew, and Esau begged for a meal. In exchange, Jacob demanded the birthright that belonged to the firstborn son. Foolish Esau "despised his birthright" by selling it to Jacob. He quickly struck the fatal bargain, sealing it with an oath. He greedily gulped down the food, wiped his mouth, rubbed his stomach, and "rose and went his way" (v. 34).

The birthright included the privilege and responsibility of governing the tribe and serving as its priest. Certain material advantages attached to the birthright, also, but the chief values of the birthright were spiritual. Esau cared nothing for these. His heart was far from the God of his fathers. He lived for the immediate, not for the ultimate. He lived for the flesh, not for the spirit. He is the progenitor of those "whose god is their belly" (Phil. 3:19, KJV).

To place highest value on the gratification of physical appetites is to deny one's essential manhood. It is his spirit, his capacity for fellowship with God, that distinguishes man from animals. Deny the spirit and you reduce people to the level of sophisticated animals, to apes and asses. By this blasphemous reduction their Maker is insulted, and they are degraded.

Jesus told the story of a rich man who talked to his soul as if it were his stomach: "eat, drink, be merry." God called the man "Fool!" (Luke 12:16-21).

What it means to be truly human is revealed in the story of the temptation of Jesus. He had fasted 40 days and was hungry. The devil said, "If you are the Son of God, command these stones to become loaves of bread." But Jesus brought physical appetite under the rule of spiritual responsibility, replying, "It is written, 'Man shall not live by bread alone, but by every word that proceeds from the mouth of God'" (Matt. 4:3-4). To be man is to place soul above stomach in the scale of values. Esau reduced himself to an animal.

II. ESAU BARGAINED HIS FUTURE FOR HIS PRESENT

Exercise of the birthright privileges awaited the death of his father. Appetite clamored for immediate satisfaction. Exaggerating the situation, Esau said, "I am about to die; of what use is a birthright to me?" (Gen. 25:32). All that mattered to him was the immediate moment.

In the family of Isaac the birthright made its possessor the carrier of the covenant between God and Abraham. The purpose of God was to bring blessing upon the entire world through the seed of Abraham. Ultimately, that covenant would produce the Bible and the Savior. What a privilege it was to play a part in the fulfillment of such a covenant! But Esau regarded this privilege with contempt. He set more value on a plateful of food in the present moment.

Scripture tells us that Esau later regretted his insane bargain, but though he wept over his loss, there was no way to reverse his actions and recover his birthright (Heb. 12:16-17). In sane moments we may perceive the stupidity of profane living, but we can never undo the damaging consequences of that folly.

You are more than a stomach to be fed. Life is more than the fleeting present moment. You are endowed by creation with a capacity for communion with God. That communion, uninterrupted by sin, can be your blessed future. Do not despise your birthright. Do not make a bowl of stew the price tag of your ruined soul. Remember, "He who sows to his own flesh will from the flesh reap corruption; but he who sows to the Spirit will from the Spirit reap eternal life" (Gal. 6:8).

Turn now from your sins. God offers you in Jesus Christ a full and free forgiveness. He offers you new life in the Spirit. He offers you the grandest birthright of all: "the inheritance of the saints in light" (Col. 1:12).

*　*　*

Do not despise your birthright. Do not live like an animal. Be a man, be a woman, be fully and truly human. Live for God and eternity. Live, as did Jesus, "by every word that proceeds from the mouth of God."

56

15

A Man of Peace

Here is a single sentence that nicely typifies the whole life of Isaac, the son of Abraham:

> *And he moved from there and dug another well, and over that they did not quarrel* (Gen. 26:22).

Isaac was less colorful than his father, Abraham, or his son Jacob. Beside their careers his own life seems quite dull. Some men are famous for their exploits, others live well but quietly. Isaac was the latter type. Nevertheless, his life and his place in God's purposes were important, and Isaac has some things to teach us.

I. ISAAC WAS A MAN OF WEALTH

He not only inherited wealth from Abraham but also gained increasing wealth by his own labors as God was pleased to prosper them. We read of him that "Isaac sowed in that land, and reaped in the same year a hundredfold. The Lord blessed him . . . he became very wealthy [in] flocks and herds" and servants (vv. 12-14).

Wealth is not evil in and of itself. It can be acquired in evil ways and employed for evil ends, but that does not make wealth wrong in itself. It was God who prospered Isaac. The secret of his success is summed up in the brief and simple statement, "The Lord blessed him."

God will have two questions to ask us in the judgment about our money: How did you get it? How did you use it? The amount is beside the point.

No one has ever improved on John Wesley's preaching on the subject of money. He advised, "Make all you can." Be industrious. "Save all you can." Be thrifty. "Give all you can." Use your material resources to relieve human misery.

It is not wrong to be wealthy, if money is honestly earned, if money is charitably used. But if we gain our wealth by exploiting others, and if we withhold our wealth from helping others, money will be our damnation.

II. ISAAC WAS ALSO A MAN OF PEACE

Because of Isaac's wealth "the Philistines envied him" (v. 14). Out of malice they stopped up the wells that had been dug by Isaac's father, filling them with earth.

Isaac patiently "dug again the wells of water." As soon as a well was flowing again, "the herdsmen of Gerar" contended against the herdsmen of Isaac for possession and control of the water. Instead of taking advantage of his wealth to war against them, Isaac preferred to move on and dig another well. He finally wore out their hostility and dug a well for which "they did not quarrel." He called it "Rehoboth," which means "broad places" or "room," for at last the Lord had made room for him to live in peace (vv. 18-22).

In a world filled with strife and violence, we need more people like Isaac. A college professor at whose feet I sat for two years used to say, "If you cannot get along with folks, just get along down the road." That was Isaac's philosophy, and his neighbors had to confess, "You are now the blessed of the Lord" (v. 29).

And that brings us to the most important thing about Isaac.

III. ISAAC WAS A MAN OF GOD

Prosperous and at peace with his neighbors, Isaac did not forget the Source of his good fortune. When God appeared to him, renewing the covenant promises that were first made with Abraham, Isaac "built an altar there and called upon the name of the Lord" (vv. 24-25).

Isaac had an altar where he offered himself and all that he possessed to God. Above his wealth and peace he valued his communion with God.

Serving God did not mean exemption from trouble and sorrow. Isaac's life would become filled with grief. His wife and son Jacob would conspire to deceive him. His other son, Esau, would deliberately marry women of Canaan to spite him. In old age, blindness and other infirmities would leave him at the mercy of scheming people. But through it all, Isaac would persist in his devotion to God. Later generations would know that God was "the God of Abraham, *Isaac*, and Jacob."

Isaac serves to remind us that wealth and peace are not the most important assets in life. What matters above all things is our relationship to God, our place in God's ongoing purposes in the world.

* * *

I do not ask you today about the size of your bank account. I do not ask you about the serenity of your life. Wealth and peace, obtained at the price of a good conscience, are not assets. They are weights that drag the soul down to hell. But even where they can be secured without moral compromise, they are never a person's greatest assets. They are incidental, not essential, to one's character and destiny.

And so I press upon you the foremost question of all: "Is your heart right with God?" Unless you can answer yes to that question, your money is a curse, and your peace is merely sedation. Are you a man or woman of God? That is all that finally matters.

16

Beth-el

Jacob was on the lam. He had deceived his father, taking advantage of old Isaac's blindness. He had cheated his brother, preying upon Esau's weakness. Now he was under a death threat from angry Esau, and he fled from home to save his skin.

On his first night out as a fugitive, Jacob pillowed his head on a stone and fell asleep. He had a strange dream, a dream that served as a medium of revelation. God came and spoke to fleeing Jacob.

If God ever speaks to some men, He will have to catch them asleep first. They are so busy and distracted when awake, so concentrated on profit and pleasure, that they cannot hear God speak. Is that true of you?

The content of Jacob's dream is simply and tersely described:

> And he dreamed that there was a ladder set up on the earth, and the top of it reached to heaven; and behold, the angels of God were ascending and descending on it! And behold, the Lord stood above it and said, "I am the Lord, the God of Abraham your father and the God of Isaac . . . Behold, I am with you and will keep you wherever you go" (Gen. 28:12-13, 15).

Here is the record of

I. A SURPRISING PLACE

The dream was full of surprises for Jacob, and when he awoke, he called the place Beth-el, "the house of God . . . the gate of heaven" (v. 17). Every life needs a Beth-el, a place where God meets with a man or a woman in personal, gracious, redeeming encounter.

A church building is the house of God only when such encounters take place. The house of God is anywhere such meetings happen. For Saul of Tarsus, enemy of Christ and persecutor of the Church, it was a spot on the road to Damascus. For the Philippian jailer, it was a dungeon where the apostles had been unjustly imprisoned. For Zacchaeus, it was a sycamore tree and a dining table. For you it may be your home, your car, some street corner—anywhere the Lord confronts you with His promise and power of salvation. Where you are right now, reading this message, can be Beth-el if you believe.

Beth-el was a place of surprise. Jacob did not expect to meet God there. "Surely the Lord is in this place," he exclaimed, "and I did not know it" (v. 16). Where Isaac worshiped, Jacob would have expected God to be present. At home, where his father prayed and stories of his grandfather's exploits of faith were told, Jacob would not have been surprised to find God present. How prone we are to limit God to "holy" places where "holy" people worship. But God is able to confront us wherever we are, making himself known in a way that excites fear and awakens love.

Jacob was learning that you can flee from the Esaus you have wronged, but you cannot escape the God against whom you have sinned. He is the ever-present Witness to all our wrongdoing, ready to break into our consciousness and call us to accountability. Trying to run from God is the most futile exercise any man has ever taken.

Here in a surprising place, Jacob experienced

II. AN AMAZING GRACE

To Jacob's surprise heaven and earth were joined. A ladder reached from the desert floor to heaven. Traffic flowed over that ladder between God and man.

In the opening chapter of John's Gospel, a man named Nathanael confesses Jesus Christ as "Son of God" and "King of Israel." And Jesus said, "Truly, truly, I say to you, you will see heaven opened, and the angels of God ascending and descending upon the Son of man" (vv. 49, 51). Jesus Christ is Jacob's ladder. In Him, God has come to us. In Him, Godhead and manhood are united, heaven and earth are joined. By means of Him our prayers ascend to God, and God's mercies descend to us. He is the "one mediator between God and men" (1 Tim. 2:5), the One through whom God saves us from sin and reconciles us to himself.

Beth-el was a place of grace. The Lord came to Jacob; Jacob did not seek the Lord. The encounter was initiated by God, not by man. The holy God broke in upon an unholy man, a guilty sinner whose very name stamped him as a crook, a usurper of others' rights. With this sinful man God renewed the Abrahamic covenant, and He promised to keep, bless, and prosper Jacob. To that divine grace Jacob made this response: "The Lord shall be my God" (Gen. 28:21).

God comes to us before we ever think of coming to Him. That is the whole meaning of grace. That is the meaning of the incarnation, crucifixion, and resurrection of Christ. In love, God has entered into our desperate situation. He has come to save the lost.

God comes to you now in Jesus Christ. He offers you forgiveness of sins and newness of life. He offers you an inheritance greater than any earthly Promised Land—a place in heaven forever! And this He offers because He loves sinners and desires to save them from guilt, bondage, and destruction. He is the God of grace.

The place where you respond in faith, where you take this God to be your God, becomes Beth-el—the gate of heaven. Through that gate you can go to Him and share His eternal life. Amazing grace indeed!

17

What Is Your Name?

Jacob wrestled with "a man" who turned out to be the Lord—one of the strange, mystical experiences recorded in the Old Testament. From his divine adversary Jacob sought a blessing, sought it with dogged tenacity, saying, "I will not let you go, unless you bless me." When he requested that blessing, the Lord asked,

> "What is your name?" And he said, "Jacob" (Gen. 32:27).

As we learn from this old story, let us begin by observing

I. THE NAME CONFESSED

"Identify yourself" meant admit the truth about yourself. Jacob's name—meaning supplanter, heel-grasper, usurper of another's rights—was shorthand for his character and behavior. All the greed of his heart and the duplicity of his life were bound up in that name—all the scheming, cheating, and lying that had marred his relationships with others.

If we want the Lord to save us from our sins, the first condition He imposes is an honest confession of who we are and what we have done. "He who conceals his transgressions will not prosper, but he who confesses and forsakes them will obtain mercy" (Prov. 28:13). The denial of our sins will imprison us in those sins. The confession of our sins is the first step toward freedom.

The name confessed became

II. THE NAME CHANGED

As the outcome of this strange encounter, Jacob's name was changed. The divine Wrestler said, "Your name shall no more be called Jacob, but Israel, for you have striven with God and with men, and have prevailed" (Gen. 32:28). The new name symbolized a new heart, a new life, a new relationship to God and to people. It carried blessed implications of gracious forgiveness, cleansing, and renewal.

By the grace of God we can all be changed. No one is trapped forever in his sins who will turn to God in sincere repentance and with an honest prayer for pardon. The glory of God is revealed in His saving love. He delights to take us as we are and make us what we ought to be. His grace to us in Jesus Christ is the promise of new life.

To an old man Jesus said, "You must be born anew" (John 3:7). A man can spend a lifetime getting lost, but he is found in the moment he surrenders his heart to Jesus Christ. A new name is "written down in glory" when a sinner is forgiven.

The name confessed and changed has become

III. THE NAME COPIED

"What is your name?" Jacob bears three names in the Bible stories about him. There is the name his parents gave him—"Jacob." There is also the name he gave himself, a name stolen from his brother and used to deceive his blind father—"Esau." And there is the name given to him by the Lord—"Israel," his royal name.

In a sense, everyone has three names. They stand for what others think about us, for what we say about ourselves, and for what God knows about us.

"Jacob." That was his *real* name. A name identifies one as an individual. Our names mark us off from all others. They stand for what we are and what we do. Call a person's name, and people summon memories of his words and deeds, the moral tenor of his life.

And we have all been "Jacob"; we have all been self-centered, grasping, and devious. We have taken advantage of others, enhancing ourselves at their expense, preying on their weakness, ignorance, or guilt. The Bible makes no bones about our guilt, saying bluntly, "All have sinned and fall short of the glory of God" (Rom. 3:23).

"Esau." That was a *false* name, adopted to deceive his father and to steal his brother's rightful blessing. Have we not all been Esaus? Have we not put on masks, pretending to be other and better than we really were, in order to protect ourselves or to exploit others?

To the Christians of his day the apostle Paul wrote, "Let love be genuine" (Rom. 12:9). So corrupt is human nature, so selfish is human life, that we are constantly tempted to deceive where even the highest and noblest of emotions, motives, and actions are concerned. We put a false face on love, pretending to care for others in order to enrich ourselves by robbing them. God only knows how often the words "I love you" have been a lever used to gain sex, or votes, or money, or promotion, or some response viewed by the pretender as another rung on the ladder of success.

"Israel." That was a *new* name, given by the One who knew Jacob best yet loved him most. Esau had been deceived, Isaac had been hoodwinked, but God knew exactly what Jacob's heart and life were like. No one pulls the wool over God's eyes. There is one Witness to every sin, a Witness who cannot be fooled, bribed, or intimidated. And that Witness is also our Judge, making it impossible to sin with impunity. This whole wrestling match occurred as Jacob sought help from God to face Esau, who was coming to meet him with 400 armed men. Sooner or later we have to face our wrongs.

Despite our sins and guilt, God loves us. In His love He makes provision to deliver us from sin. He can change our hearts and lives and futures. He can radically alter our characters and destinies. This patient, redeeming love brought into history our Lord Jesus Christ, the true Israel, who died for our sins and rose again for our pardon. If we confess and forsake our sins, if we face up to the truth about ourselves, if we take off the false faces and cast away deceit, we can be forgiven and changed through Christ.

The first time Jesus saw Simon Peter, He said to him, "You are Simon . . . you shall be called Cephas" (John 1:42). You are . . . you shall be! He accepts us as we are, lost and ruined sinners. And He makes us what we should be, the forgiven, renewed, and adopted children of God! Your name, your life, your relationship to God and others, can be changed!

What is *your* name?

18

From Crook to Prince

Through most of his life Jacob had been "as crooked as a dog's hind leg," to borrow an old saying. He was a born deceiver and a practiced opportunist. He proved to be a consummate confidence man, always using people to his own advantage.

Twice he took advantage of his own family, exploiting Esau's weakness to steal his birthright, and exploiting Isaac's blindness to steal Esau's blessing. He fled from home to keep his outraged brother from killing him.

Now he is coming back home—older, wiser, and richer. It was on the trip back home that the strange wrestling match occurred between Jacob and "a man" who was also somehow God. Toward daybreak Jacob's assailant spoke these words:

> Your name shall no more be called Jacob, but Israel, for you have striven with God and with men, and have prevailed (Gen. 32:28).

Let's take a closer look at this man who experienced such a radical change in his life.

I. JACOB WAS A MAN TRAPPED BY HIS PAST

As he journeyed homeward, he was told that Esau was coming to meet him with 400 men—a small army. "Then Jacob was greatly afraid and distressed" (vv. 6-7). The last person in the world that Jacob was prepared to meet was the brother against whom he had sinned so deeply.

As Billy Sunday used to preach, "Chickens come home to roost." Our sins find us out. Sooner or later the law of sowing and reaping brings us to the harvesttime.

Time is irreversible. We cannot undo what we have done, however much we may regret those past deeds. As Pilate said of the placard affixed to the cross of Jesus, "What I have written I have written" (John 19:22). You cannot undo your misdeeds.

Time is irreversible and judgment is inescapable. Somehow, sometime, somewhere the past catches up with us, and we must bear the consequences of our wrongdoing. This is a moral universe, and its laws break all who break its laws. Wherever a Jacob cheats and steals, sooner or later an Esau comes to meet him.

II. JACOB WAS A MAN HELPLESS IN HIS PRESENT

There was nowhere to hide. The "artful dodger" had no tricks left in his bag. He could no longer depend upon his cunning and conniving. There was no way ahead and no way back.

At that point Jacob did the only wise thing possible. He humbled his heart and prayed. He cast himself upon the mercy of God, saying,

> *I am not worthy of the least of all the steadfast love and all the faithfulness which thou hast shown to thy servant . . . Deliver me, I pray thee, from the hand of my brother* (Gen. 32:10-11).

Where sin is concerned, there is just one hope—the mercy of God. And the truest thing about us all is our deep unworthiness. We have sinned against God and against one another, and we deserve only the wrath of God. But God is merciful! He takes delight in pardoning our sins and in changing our lives.

That blessed fact brings us to the happiest note struck in the Old Testament story of Jacob.

III. JACOB WAS A MAN FREED FOR HIS FUTURE

His name was changed, and his life was changed. He is no more the deceiver, the supplanter. He becomes, instead, a prince with God. He limped away from his encounter with God a chastened, forgiven, and changed man.

Evidence of Jacob's changed heart is supplied when he meets Esau. Instead of battling, they embrace, hugging one another and weeping for joy. Jacob then urges upon his brother a huge peace offering, saying, "Accept, I pray you, my gift that is brought to you, because God has dealt graciously with me, and because I have enough" (33:11). "I have enough"! When a con man says that, you know that repentance and new life have occurred!

Now Jacob is free at last. He is not bound by his former sins or by the deceitful nature that produced them. He can enter upon his future as a new person, marked by spiritual royalty. He is free to be unselfish and generous, free to trust God and serve people.

* * *

God's mercy breaks the grip of the past upon our lives. His forgiveness creates a new situation, and we are freed to become the instruments of His purpose. There is nothing so liberating as His pardoning love. He gives us, by grace, a future and a hope.

Like Jacob, to experience that future, we must face the truth and confess our sins. We must admit that our name is Jacob before God can change it to Israel. "If we confess our sins, he is faithful and just, and will forgive our sins and cleanse us from all unrighteousness" (1 John 1:9). Trapped by an accusing past, helpless in the menacing present, we can nevertheless be freed for the glorious future that God has prepared for those who love and serve Him.

19

Slain Dreamers, Living Dreams

Here comes this dreamer. ... Let us kill him ... and we shall see what will become of his dreams (Gen. 37:19-20).

These are the words of Joseph's brothers. They hated Joseph. He had dreamed strange things—dreamed of ruling over his family and receiving their homage. When he told them his dreams, they were contemptuous and angry toward their kid brother. Arrogant pup! Did he really think they would ever bow their knees to him? Jealousy and hatred festered in their hearts, and they sought opportunity to destroy him.

I. THE DREAMER WAS TESTED

Joseph's dreams were from God. This is how God works. When He wants to change things in the world, He plants a dream in the heart of some man or woman. God does not ride roughshod over society, compelling change with a bloody sword. That is how we try to improve our situations, and violence breeds more violence, death spawns more death. God is wiser and better—He enables a man to dream and to suffer for the dream.

Aye, suffer! Our world is rough on dreamers. We do not hail their dreams with joy. We have proud egos and vested interests to protect. We have our own plans for our lives, and if God-given dreams threaten our wishes, let the dreamer beware!

Joseph was not slain by his brothers. He was spared through the intervention of one brother, but he was sold as a slave to a passing caravan of foreign traders. And then he was resold, and framed by a lying woman, and flung into an Egyptian dungeon, where he languished in lonely misery.

Abraham Lincoln dreamed of a union preserved and a race liberated from slavery. For those dreams he prayed and labored with increasing resolution and devotion. No American leader was more vilified than he, and finally he was cut down by a crazed assassin's bullet.

Jesus Christ dreamed the grandest dreams of all. He dreamed of people from all nations and races delivered from sin, reconciled to God, and living at peace with one another. He dreamed of a kingdom without frontiers, a society eternal in duration, righteous in character, loving in behavior. He dreamed of the conquest of sin, sorrow, and suffering. His exposition of that dream was given in these words:

> *The Spirit of the Lord is upon me, because he has anointed me to preach good news to the poor. He has sent me to proclaim release to the captives and recovering of sight to the blind, to set at liberty those who are oppressed, to proclaim the acceptable year of the Lord* (Luke 4:18-19).

To that dream Jesus devoted His time and effort. "He went about doing good, and healing all that were oppressed by the devil, for God was with him" (Acts 10:38). God was with Him, but men were against Him. His dream set Him on a collision course with the political and religious leaders of His day. With fangs bared, they bayed on His trail relentlessly, finally hounding Him to a lonely, bloody cross, where He died praying for His merciless tormentors: "Father, forgive them; for they know not what they do" (Luke 23:34).

Yes, the dreamer was tested, but

II. THE DREAM WAS TRIUMPHANT

You can kill the dreamers, but you cannot slay their dreams. Sooner or later the dreams given by God will be fulfilled. And when the dreams come true, the very people who oppressed, abused, and slew the dreamers become their beneficiaries. When Joseph's dreams were realized, his honored position saved his family from famine and starvation.

Our sins were the nails that spiked Jesus to the Cross. Yet that Cross became our liberation from the most galling of all bondage, our slavery to sin and guilt. The love of God was stronger than death, and Jesus rose from the grave with power to implement His dreams. He comes to us, willing the noblest and best for us. He comes to us to offer new life, true life, in which our nightmares vanish and His dreams come true. When we yield to His pardoning and renewing love, we discover the freedom, peace, and joy we vainly sought in the world.

"Here comes this dreamer"! We crucified Him, but He triumphed over our misguided hatred and envy. And His dreams are coming true. Beyond the bloody mess that we call human history lies the ultimate triumph of the Cross. In his dreams and visions of the future, John heard "loud voices in heaven, saying, 'The kingdom of the world has become the kingdom of our Lord and of his Christ, and he shall reign for ever and ever.'" And John heard also "the voice of a great multitude," like the sound of thundering cataracts, saying, "Hallelujah! For the Lord our God the Almighty reigns" (Rev. 11:15; 19:6). You can count on it—the dreams of Jesus Christ are deathless and invincible.

*   *   *

You can be part of that conquering dream. You can share the future of Jesus Christ. You can live in this world as His forgiven disciple, and you can live in the world to come as His liberated servant—beyond sin, pain, death, and grief forever!

20

The Intercessor

Joseph was sold into slavery by his brothers, then resold in Egypt by those who first bought him. There his life hit bottom. He was cast into prison on false charges of attempted rape.

But God brought him from a dungeon to a throne. He became second in power to Pharaoh himself. Now the brothers of Joseph are before him, buying food to survive the famine in Canaan. They do not know that the one who has them in his power is the very brother they so terribly wronged.

Joseph has tricked his brothers. Evidence of theft was planted in Benjamin's food sack. Joseph tells them all to return home except Benjamin. He is to remain in Egypt as Joseph's servant.

At this point in the story Judah emerges as a magnificent intercessor. He pleads for the release of his younger brother and offers to become a slave in his place. Loss of the youngest child, argues Judah, will bring their father down "with sorrow to the grave" (Gen. 44:29, KJV), for "his life is bound up in the lad's life" (v. 30). Judah's moving appeal closes with these poignant words:

For how can I go back to my father if the lad is not with me? I fear to see the evil that would come upon my father (v. 34).

The intercession of Judah melted the heart of Joseph. "He wept aloud" as he "made himself known to his brothers" (45:2, 1). All the brothers were forgiven, and the whole family of Jacob was invited to dwell in Egypt, where Joseph could make them secure during the continuing famine.

Let us look briefly at the intercession made by Judah. First of all we see that

I. JUDAH'S INTERCESSION LAID BARE HIS FATHER'S HEART

He had come to know how deeply Jacob loved his sons. The old man still grieved for Joseph, whom he thought dead for many years. His affection now rested upon his "little one" (44:20, KJV), Benjamin, thought to be the only surviving child of Jacob's favorite wife, Rachel. The lives of father and son were inseparably entwined. If Benjamin were lost to him, Jacob would find no consolation this side of the grave.

Let me say it reverently and firmly: If you and I could know how deeply God loves His children, we could never consent to wrong them, and we would never cease to pray for them. We do not know how to value people until we see how much they mean to God. He is their Maker and Redeemer, and His love for them makes them precious above all things.

God's love has been disclosed in the cross of Christ. That is how much He cares for us all. A man may be ever so poor, ever so ignorant, ever so diseased, ever so wicked, and yet God's life has been bound up with that man's life! The love of the Father should bind us together, so that compassion and intercession become native to our hearts.

Yes, Judah's intercession exposed his father's heart.

II. JUDAH'S INTERCESSION LAID BARE HIS OWN HEART ALSO

Not only had he come to know his father better, but also he had learned something about himself and his brothers.

It was Judah who, many years before, had urged the sale of Joseph into slavery. It was he who said, "Come, let us sell him to the Ishmaelites" (37:27). Now he pleads that Benjamin may not become a slave, indentured to an alien. Judah has come to place a higher value upon the privilege and responsibility of brotherhood. He has become less self-centered, more concerned for others.

Indeed, Judah now prefers to suffer rather than inflict suffering. He is willing to be a servant that another may be free. He is ready to risk his own life in order to rescue the life of another. Hear his stirring, unselfish plea: "Let your servant, I pray you, remain instead of the lad as a slave to my lord; and let the lad go back with his brothers" (v. 33).

When God's love changes our hearts, we will place others above ourselves. We will be ready to suffer and to sacrifice in order to serve their welfare. Looking out for No. 1 is the way of the wicked. Bearing one another's burdens is the way of the redeemed (Gal. 6:2). The grace of God changes the persecutor into an intercessor.

Look around you. Who needs your love, your help, your prayers today? Who needs you to plead their cause? Who needs you to come to their rescue? Have you joined the ranks of the transformed intercessors? It is the most satisfying life possible, for it is the most Christlike life possible.

Aye, Christlike! Jesus Christ is a brother who knows the Father's love for the least of His children, and who prays for them, that they might be saved from sin's bondage and united for life with the Father.

*   *   *

Friend, He loves you. He prays for you. He makes your freedom a glorious possibility. He is the divine Judah, who intercedes for you. He is the divine Joseph, who offers you forgiveness and fellowship. Come to Him, trust in Him, and you will truly live—now and forever!

21

God's Good Intentions

Joseph, speaking to his brothers, summed up his trials and triumphs in these words:

> *You meant evil against me; but God meant it for good* (Gen. 50:20).

He did not arrive at this conclusion easily. There were times when he must have felt that even God had forsaken him. But his faith endured, and his perspective matured, until he could see how God had used the evil intentions of men to further, unwittingly, His own good purposes.

The story of Joseph, which occupies over a dozen chapters in the Book of Genesis, can be summed up in three words—dreams, dungeon, and diadem. God bestowed upon Joseph

I. THE GIFT OF DREAMS

Joseph was gifted by God to interpret dreams, both his own and others'. He dreamed of occupying a position of such power that his parents and his brothers bowed before him. These dreams, when he related them, aroused their jealousy and rage. In retaliation, the brothers sold him as a slave, and he was taken to Egypt.

There he prospered, for "the Lord was with Joseph" (39:2). That initial prosperity, however, was rudely shattered. His master's wife tried in vain to get Joseph into her bed. Badly mistreated and sorely tempted, how easily the virile young slave might have yielded! But he spurned her proffered body, saying, "How . . . can I do this great wickedness, and sin against God?" (v. 9). Joseph's integrity makes hypocrites of all who plead their circumstances as an excuse for sin.

The dreamer was soon acquainted with

II. THE GLOOM OF A DUNGEON

The rejected and frustrated woman framed innocent Joseph with false charges of attempted rape. He was cast into prison, and there he languished, forgotten by men whom he had helped and apparently forgotten by God whom he had honored.

But "the Lord was with Joseph" (v. 21), and he was later summoned from the dungeon to interpret strange dreams that troubled the mind of Pharaoh. Pleased with his service, Pharaoh wisely promoted Joseph to the post of economic administrator. "He set him over all the land of Egypt" (41:43), second in power to Pharaoh himself. In choosing Joseph for this responsibility, and in showering him with honors and wealth, Pharaoh put his finger on the secret of Joseph's integrity and success: "Can we find such a man as this in whom is the Spirit of God?" (v. 38).

The wisdom of Joseph prepared Egypt to survive a seven-year famine. In Canaan no such provision had been made, for the family of Joseph had gotten rid of the troubling dreamer. Forced to enter Egypt to purchase food, the brothers of Joseph were shocked and alarmed to find themselves at the mercy of the one against whom they had so deeply sinned.

In a touching scene, Joseph freely forgave them. "He kissed all his brothers and wept upon them; and after that his brothers talked with him" (45:15). Forgiveness opened the door to fellowship.

The faithful Joseph now experienced

III. THE GLORY OF A DIADEM

His dream was fulfilled. He occupied the position of power that God had chosen for him, and before him all his family bowed, dependent upon him as their savior.

The path to the throne had led through slavery and prison. Some of the turns in the road had puzzled Joseph as he made the journey, but he kept trusting God and pursuing the dream. In his dealings with his brothers, Joseph spoke the truth that lay beneath the harsh circumstances through which he had passed:

> It was not you who sent me here, but God ... As for you, you meant evil against me; but God meant it for good, to bring it about that many people should be kept alive, as they are today (Gen. 45:8; 50:20).

God had purposes larger than Joseph's sufferings. He made Joseph, precisely through those misfortunes, the savior of a family and a nation. And through that covenant nation, saved by Joseph's intervention, God carried on His plan to give the world a Savior. Out of Israel came Jesus Christ!

Come with me across a span of centuries. A greater than Joseph is rejected by His brothers: "He came to his own home, and his own people received him not" (John 1:11). He too is given a mock trial based on lying charges: "The whole council sought false testimony against Jesus, that they might put him to death" (Matt. 26:59). Unlike Joseph, however, He is not merely flung into prison. He is condemned, tortured, and executed:

> *Pilate, wishing to satisfy the crowd, . . . having scourged Jesus, . . . delivered him to be crucified. And the soldiers led him away . . . and plaiting a crown of thorns they put it on him. . . . And they struck his head . . . spat upon him . . . mocked him . . . And they crucified him* (Mark 15:15-17, 19-20, 24).

But God had sent Him there, and God meant it for good, to keep many people alive. God raised Jesus from the dead, thereby declaring Him to be Savior and Lord. To those who rejected Him, to His crucifiers, and to us, the Good News came: "God, having raised up his servant, sent him to you . . . to bless you in turning every one of you from your wickedness" (Acts 3:26).

Jesus Christ freely forgives our sins when we cast ourselves upon His mercy. And He invites us into the grandest fellowship ever enjoyed, making himself an intimate friend in our daily lives.

I invite you to come to Him and find new life today!

22

A Great Forgiver

Joseph is one of the strongest characters in the Bible. He was like one of those spring-mounted punching bags—no matter how hard he was hit, he always bounced back.

He took some hard blows, blows that would have made lots of men bitter. His own brothers, angry and jealous, sold him into slavery. As a slave he was falsely accused by a lying, frustrated woman and thrown into prison. In prison he helped a man who quickly forgot him when released from prison and restored to the king's favor.

But through all of this Joseph refused to give up. He stayed true to God and to his own ideals. And in the course of time, and in the providence of God, Joseph was made ruler over Egypt, second in command to Pharaoh himself. His gift of wisdom saved the nation from famine, and he became as well the savior of his own undeserving brothers.

When those brothers found themselves at the mercy of the one they had so viciously wronged, they were filled with terror. They confessed their guilt and begged Joseph to forgive and spare them. The response of Joseph is one of the most magnificent passages in Scripture.

Joseph said to them, "Fear not, for am I in the place of God? As for you, you meant evil against me; but God meant it for good, to bring it about that many people should be kept alive, as they are today. So do not fear; I will provide for you and your little ones." Thus he reassured them and comforted them (Gen. 50:19-21).

This is not just ancient history. God would teach us some vital lessons from this portion of the Bible.

I. JOSEPH'S LIFE REMINDS US THAT ATTITUDES ARE MORE IMPORTANT THAN CIRCUMSTANCES

In your sufferings have you become bitter? In your sufferings have you become a quitter? You cannot excuse your moral failures by pointing to your physical or material circumstances. Joseph proves that a man can live a good life in a bad situation. He can be true to God under the pressure of strong and persistent temptation. He can be abused, slandered, imprisoned, and still maintain his integrity. He can cling to his faith when the face of God seems to be hidden from him.

When Potiphar's wife, strongly attracted to the Hebrew slave, kept begging Joseph to climb into bed with her, his reply was, "How . . . can I do this great wickedness, and sin against God?" (39:9). Because he was steadfastly loyal to God in slavery and in prison, we read that "the Lord was with Joseph" (v. 21).

The Lord did not spare him from suffering, but through suffering He molded Joseph into the kind of man he needed to lead the people during disastrous times. Great souls are forged in the furnace of affliction. They demonstrate that attitudes are more important than circumstances.

We cannot always choose our circumstances, but we can and do choose our attitudes. What happens to you is often decided by persons and forces beyond your control. How you respond to what happens is your own decision. And it is that response, not the events themselves, that determines your character and destiny.

II. JOSEPH'S LIFE ALSO REMINDS US THAT FORGIVENESS IS BETTER THAN VENGEANCE

When someone hurts you, how do you respond? Do you become filled with hatred? Do you plot to take revenge? Do you begin to live for the day when you have the upper hand and can return evil for evil? Nothing is more self-destructive than the passion for revenge. It poisons the springs of thought and action until all life's good things are spoiled and wasted.

When those who had hated him most and had treated him worst were in Joseph's hands, he did not avenge himself. Instead, he wept over them, freely forgave them, and promised to help them. No wonder Joseph has been called "the most Christlike character in the Old Testament." His magnificent act of forgiveness makes us think of Jesus, hanging on the Cross before a jeering mob and praying, "Father, forgive them; for they know not what they do" (Luke 23:34).

When we forgive others, it may not always liberate them, but it certainly frees us. An unforgiving spirit is the forger of chains and prisons. It holds a person captive to the basest and cruelest and most enslaving passions of twisted personality. It corrodes the thought and desolates the life of the one who will not forgive. The healing of our inner lives demands that we forgive those who have wronged us. Joseph is witness to the truth that great sufferers can be great forgivers.

To say "I am sorry" when we have wronged others, or to say "I forgive" when others have wronged us, is to speak liberating words—assuming the words are sincere, are from the heart. To bear grudges, to exact revenge, to refuse to forgive offenders is to enclose your spirit in a steel cage, an unlit and lonely prison. An ounce of pardon is better than a pound of flesh.

*   *   *

Joseph speaks to us across the centuries. His life says to us, Do not let circumstances govern you. Attitudes are more important. Do not allow vengefulness to poison your heart. Forgiveness brings healing. You can miss all that God planned to accomplish through your life if you knuckle under to trouble or if you nourish hatred. Like Joseph, live in the confidence that God works all things together for the good of those who love Him.

23

Growing in Bloody Soil

When Joseph was prime minister of Egypt, his people set-tled there to escape famine in Canaan. As time passed, the children of Israel multiplied and prospered—"the land was filled with them" (Exod. 1:7).

Everything changes, and politics most of all. Joseph died and decades became centuries. "A new king" rose to power in Egypt "who did not know Joseph" (v. 8).

Fearing the growing strength of these resident aliens, this Pharaoh enslaved the Israelites. Their lives became "bit-ter with hard service" (v. 14). The ancient record says, how-ever,

> *The more they were oppressed, the more they multiplied* (v. 12).

Here is a principle often demonstrated in history: You cannot destroy those whom God intends to save and use for His own purposes.

I. A SUFFERING ISRAEL HAS PROVED INDESTRUCTIBLE

Israel has known suffering that defies description. Across the centuries, in country after country, pogroms and persecutions have befallen this people. The worst of all attempts to annihilate them was the holocaust that raged in the gas ovens of Hitler's concentration camps during World War II. Six million Jews, shipped like cattle to these camps, were systematically and ruthlessly destroyed.

Nevertheless, Israel survives. Other ancient people have disappeared, but Israel persists as a molding force in world history. God is not through with Israel, and no ruler, no country, no army can exterminate those whom God wills to sustain in existence.

Jacob is frail—a "worm," the prophet Isaiah said (41: 14). And Joseph is a memory, a fading reminder of better days. Pharaoh is mighty, the ruler of a world power, hailed as god over his land and to his people. But all the cruelty and craftiness of Pharaoh cannot overcome Israel—"The more they were oppressed, the more they multiplied."

Pharaoh is gone and Egypt has been eclipsed, but Israel survives and grows. Within my own lifetime I saw the great Jew-haters rise to power and sink in disgrace—Hitler, Mussolini, Stalin. They carried out their senseless, violent purges and persecutions, but they fell at last, disowned by the very fools and tools who had worshiped them. Afflicted Israel survived. The "worm" outlasted the monsters.

Centuries after Joseph died, the Christ was born. In His manhood He gathered a motley, unpromising group of disciples about Him and said to them, "In the world you have tribulation; but be of good cheer, I have overcome the world" (John 16:33).

II. A SUFFERING CHURCH HAS PROVED INDESTRUCTIBLE

From its inception the Church of Jesus Christ has been afflicted and persecuted. By prison, torture, and execution efforts were made to stamp out this movement in its infancy. But the more they were oppressed, the more they multiplied. In the first wave of persecution that broke over them, they fled from Jerusalem, the earliest center of Christian life. Did they flee to hide in silence and disappear from history? Not on your life! "Those who were scattered went about preaching the word" (Acts 8:4). "And the hand of the Lord was with them, and a great number that believed turned to the Lord" (11:21).

The Word of Christ that they proclaimed could not be jailed, could not be killed. "The word of the Lord grew and prevailed mightily" (Acts 19:20) despite the frantic efforts of the enemies of God to destroy His people. Before three centuries had passed, the Roman Empire, ruled by its human idols, unleashed a total of 10 savage persecutions against the Church of Christ. Those emperors are gone, their empire has been scattered, but the Church lives on, preaching salvation through the life, death, and resurrection of Jesus Christ.

"The blood of martyrs is the seed of the Church." That was true of Israel. That has been true of the Church throughout its history. No weapon formed against the Church has prospered. No attempt to destroy the Church has succeeded. When the iron curtain falls, the Church will still be standing. When the bamboo curtain falls, the Church will still be standing. If Western civilization collapses and democracies perish, the Church will survive. Communism cannot destroy the Church. Fascism cannot destroy the Church. "On this rock," said Jesus, "I will build my church, and the powers of death shall not prevail against it" (Matt. 16:18). You cannot destroy those whom God intends to save and use for His own purposes!

John had a vision of people from all nations standing

before the throne of God in heaven. An elder identified them: "These are they who have come out of the great tribulation." Yet they were "a great multitude which no man could number" (Rev. 7:14, 9). Great tribulation—great multitude! "The more they were oppressed, the more they multiplied."

Let those who will pour contempt upon the Church. Let those who will oppose its gospel and harass its people. The Church will survive. How comforting it is to belong to the one institution on earth that has an eternal future!

24

The Sorrowing Savior

Ancient Israel was enslaved. Life for them was hard, bitter, and degrading. Sighs and groans were pressed from their heavy hearts, and "God heard their groaning" (Exod. 2:24). The ears of God are fine-tuned to the cries of oppressed people.

God is not aloof and uncaring. He is not a heartless spectator of human misery. Listen to His words:

> *I know their sufferings, and I have come down to deliver them* (Exod. 3:7-8).

The deliverance of Israel can be summed up in three brief statements. The first is this:

I. GOD SOUGHT A MAN

God works through people to help people. He needed a shepherd to lead His people like a flock from Egypt into Canaan. For this awesome, often thankless, responsibility the Lord tapped Moses.

First, He got the man's attention. A bush blazed with fire but was not consumed. Moses turned aside to see "this great sight," and "God called to him out of the bush" (vv. 3-4).

In this dramatic episode the emphasis is placed on God's grace and power. Moses is a reluctant conscript. He views the assignment in the light of his past failures, and a sense of inadequacy unnerves him. "Who am I," he exclaims, "that I should go to Pharaoh, and bring the sons of Israel out of Egypt?" (v. 11).

God counters the objection with irresistible argument: "I will be with you" (v. 12). When God is with a man, refusal is unthinkable, and failure is impossible. Moses put the question wrongly. Looking at himself, he asked, "Who am I?" He should have looked to God and should have asked, *"Whose* am I?" It has been well said, "One man with God is a majority." A life spent in submission to God's purpose will succeed. As Bertha Munro, a valiant Christian educator, has said, "God will not waste a dedicated life."

God sought and found His man. Next we note that

II. GOD SHARED A SORROW

The grace of God, no less than His power, comes into focus in the story of Moses' call to service. He is the God who sees, who cares, and who responds to the misery of His people. "I know their sufferings, and I have come down to deliver them."

The God of the Bible is touched by human misery. He is not remote and indifferent, unseeing and unfeeling, like the idols of the pagans. He is exalted over all, but He gets involved with all. He does not turn from His suffering, weeping people with a heartless shrug, saying, "You got yourselves into this mess, you will have to get yourselves out." No! He rather says, "I have seen the affliction of my people . . . and have heard their cry . . . I know their sufferings, and I have come down to deliver them" (3:7-8).

Deliver them He did! The story of that deliverance is the heart of the Book of Exodus. And that Exodus from "the house of bondage" was the beginning of Israel's history as a nation. Out of that history came the Bible. Out of that history came Jesus Christ. And that is another story of another exodus that gives universal dimensions to the words of God: "I know their sufferings, and I have come down to deliver them."

In Jesus Christ, God had a personal experience of human suffering. Jesus Christ is the eternal Word of God incarnate. "The Word became flesh and dwelt among us" (John 1:14). God became a man, "a man of sorrows, and acquainted with grief" (Isa. 53:3). In the presence of sin and its tragic consequences, "he groaned," "he sighed," and "he wept." The tears of God fell upon the soil of Israel, and those tears were shed for the whole world.

The Son of God lived through our sorrow-producing experiences. He knew what it feels like to be misunderstood, rejected, betrayed, denied, and hated. He knew what it feels like to be weary, hungry, and lonely. He knew what it feels like to lose a friend to death, and to face the approach of death alone and disarmed. "I know their sufferings," God can say, not as a bystander but as a participant!

God shared a sorrow, and

III. God saved a people

In Jesus Christ, God came down to deliver. Moses lived to deliver his people from political bondage. Jesus died to rescue His people from spiritual slavery, to save them from sin, guilt, and death. Facing the Cross, where He would become an offering for sin, Jesus said, "My soul is very sorrowful" (Matt. 26:38). From the Cross, as He endured the torment of the damned, He exclaimed, "My God, my God, why hast thou forsaken me?" (27:46).

Yes, He came down—down to earth, down to our human agonies, down to Calvary's lonely pain and shame, down to the silence and mystery of the grave! He came to deliver. He defeated sin and death. When they had done their worst to Him, He rose again! As the risen Lord, He offers eternal life to every sinner who will repent and trust in Him. Millions have. Have you?

Before the throne of God in heaven, John beheld a host of people who had triumphed over "the beast." "And they sing the song of Moses, the servant of God, and the song of the Lamb, saying, 'Great and wonderful are thy deeds, O Lord God the Almighty!'" (Rev. 15:3). The song of Moses celebrated political freedom. The song of the Lamb celebrates spiritual freedom. These are the words of God who said, "I know their sufferings, and I have come down to deliver them."

25

The Mouth That Failed

God called Moses to lead the enslaved Israelites out of Egypt. God is too wise to wait for volunteers. He must get His work done, so He conscripts His workmen.

Moses shrank from the assignment and begged God to send someone else. Does this not make him at once a relative of ours? "I am not eloquent," was Moses' excuse; "I am slow of speech and of tongue" (Exod. 4:10).

God's anger was kindled by the unbelief of Moses. You see, the Creator expects the creature to trust His wisdom, power, and love. But as a concession to faltering Moses, God said,

> *Is there not Aaron, your brother, the Levite? I know that he can speak well . . . He shall speak for you to the people* (vv. 14, 16).

So Moses went to his task with Aaron as his spokesman. What a mistake that proved to be! Aaron became the mouth that failed.

I. AARON BECAME A MOUTH FOR RELIGIOUS COMPROMISE

While Moses communed with God on Mount Sinai, receiving there the law by which Israel was to be governed, Aaron led an ungrateful people into gross idolatry.

The people came to Aaron, saying, "Make us gods, who shall go before us" (32:1). Instead of denouncing their ingratitude and folly, Aaron caved in to their sinful clamor. He took their gold ornaments, melted them down, and shaped the molten gold into a calf. Having arrived at bad, he hurried on to worse, building an altar before the idol and proclaiming "a feast to the Lord" (v. 5).

When Moses came down from the mountain, the spectacle of an idolatrous orgy, led by Aaron, met his anguished and angry gaze. Aaron was called on the carpet to answer for the outrage and offered the lamest lying excuse on record: "I threw it [the gold] into the fire, and there came out this calf" (v. 24).

A terrible judgment fell upon the camp of Israel, and the incident closes with these sad words: "And the Lord sent a plague upon the people, because they made the calf which Aaron made" (v. 35).

We are given mouths to speak for God. We live under the constant temptation of compromising the truth in order to curry or retain the favor of those to whom we speak. This ancient story is a dramatic reminder that the end result of religious compromise is not popularity but plague.

II. AARON LATER BECAME A MOUTH FOR JEALOUS AMBITION

Aaron and his sister, Miriam, were jealous of the authority and leadership of Moses. They wanted a bigger slice of the melon for themselves. In their discontent they "spoke against Moses" (Num. 12:1), adding to the burden of the people's incessant grumbling, which Moses had to bear. Their bitter complaint is recorded in verse 2: "And they said, 'Has the Lord indeed spoken only through Moses? Has he not spoken through us also?'" Then follows a classical understatement: "And the Lord heard it."

God, who knows every human heart and hears every human word, called the two rebels to the door of the Tabernacle. There He rebuked their arrogance and vindicated Moses. As a judgment upon her, Miriam was smitten with leprosy. Aaron cried to Moses, "We have done foolishly and have sinned" (v. 11). Moses, bighearted man that he was, prayed for Miriam's healing.

Once again Aaron, as weak as he was eloquent, had opened his mouth only to make trouble for Moses.

We, too, have been summoned to function as the servants of the Word of God. In sermon, or lecture, or testimony we are to make that Word known at all cost to ourselves. Our service will be cankered and our souls will be imperiled if we allow ourselves to become jealous of the recognition that other servants are receiving and the authority they are wielding. Our mouths will fail when our message becomes, not the proclamation of the Word of God, but the outpouring of our jealous and frustrated ambition.

Let it now be said that Aaron's entire record is not negative.

III. AARON ALSO BECAME A MOUTH FOR MORAL INSTRUCTION

Aaron was chosen by God to be Israel's first high priest. As such, it became his duty to teach the law to the people.

The priesthood was bound to the law as we are to the gospel. God's solemn charge to Aaron is found in Lev. 10:8, 11: "And the Lord spoke to Aaron, saying, '. . . teach the people of Israel all the statutes which the Lord has spoken to them by Moses.'" As a pardoned sinner, Aaron was chosen by a gracious God to play an important part in the history of His covenant and people.

In Aaron's life, therefore, as in ours, the last word is the triumph of divine grace. That he has spoken foolishly, selfishly, and even wickedly does not vacate his office. God's infinite, patient mercy continues to respond to repentance with forgiveness. He wipes the mouth of a failing spokesman and says, "Now, once again, serve My people by sharing with them the word that I have given you."

"Then the word of the Lord came to Jonah the second time, saying, 'Arise, go to Nineveh, that great city, and proclaim to it the message that I tell you'" (Jonah 3:1-2). How I treasure that statement! What if God stripped us of the privilege of Kingdom service the first time we disqualified ourselves by disobedience? Think how brief would be the Christian lives and ministries of nearly all persons! God has pity upon our stupid hearts and failing mouths, and He constantly renews His pardon and our peace.

Aaron is a challenge to us all, a challenge to look to our own mouths.

Do we speak to rebuke sin, or do we knuckle under to the pressure of an idolatrous people?

Do we speak to support the servants of God, or do we grumble and criticize out of jealousy for their positions of leadership?

Do we speak to acquaint others with the Word of God, or do we stand by in silence while they stumble and perish in darkness?

The gift and power of speech carries with it an awesome responsibility. Our mouths can glorify God, or they can destroy us. Jesus said, "By your words you will be justified, and by your words you will be condemned" (Matt. 12:37).

How easy it is to misuse the power of speech. How easy it is to grumble against God and to complain against others. But what a privilege is ours to speak for God and to bear His saving words to those around us! We will be wise to pray as did the Psalmist of old:

> Let the words of my mouth and the meditation of my heart be acceptable in thy sight, O Lord, my rock and my redeemer (Ps. 19:14).

26

Liberation

Thus says the Lord, the God of Israel, "Let my people go" (Exod. 5:1).

These were the words of God, spoken by Moses and Aaron to Pharaoh, the ruler of ancient Egypt. Israel was in bondage, and God was demanding their release. God is the enemy of

I. THE OPPRESSORS

God opposes slavery. He is committed to freedom. As the Creator, He conferred freedom upon man. As the Redeemer, He restores freedom to man. Whatever enslaves and oppresses the human spirit is the enemy not only of mankind but of God.

Pharaoh arrogantly responded, "Who is the Lord, that I should heed his voice and let Israel go? I do not know the Lord, and moreover I will not let Israel go" (v. 2). Egypt had her own gods. Indeed, Pharaoh himself was deemed a god. He was defending his own turf against some upstart, alien deity. And if the God of Israel wanted to rumble, then let the fight begin!

"I do not know the Lord"! Pharaoh never spoke truer words. Had he known whom he was up against, how quickly he would have pulled in his horns and yielded to the Lord's demands. The loss of his slaves would have been a small price to pay for his throne and his life!

Instead of freeing the slaves, Pharaoh added to their sufferings. And then, like bolts of lightning from an angry heaven, judgment after judgment fell upon Egypt. Ten plagues afflicted land, cattle, and people until the groans of the Egyptians were louder than the wails of their Hebrew slaves. Pharaoh "hardened his heart" and fought back through nine bloody rounds. But in the 10th, God scored a knockout. Egypt's haughty ruler threw in the towel, crying, "Rise up, go forth from among my people . . . go, serve the Lord. . . . Take your flocks and your herds . . . and be gone" (12:31-32).

Yes, God is the enemy of slavery. And sooner or later every false god and every wicked man who opposes His demand for the freedom of His people will fall beneath His judgment.

Hunger enslaves, and God says to hunger, "Let my people go." *Disease* enslaves, and God says to disease, "Let my people go." *Ignorance* enslaves, and God says to ignorance, "Let my people go." *Poverty* enslaves, and God says to poverty, "Let my people go." God has raised up farmers, doctors, educators, engineers, economists, reformers, and apostles to pioneer the paths to liberty.

The worst of all tyrants is sin, producing guilt, shame, and death. Sin enslaves the mind, heart, and conscience of mankind. Sin destroys homes and nations. It creates liars, thieves, rapists, murderers, and hypocrites. It produces crimes, riots, and wars. It tears society apart, filling the air with screams and soaking the earth with blood. Sin in the heart is a crueler monarch than any ancient Pharaoh or than any modern dictator.

Over against the oppressors of mankind stands

II. The Liberator

To deliver us from sin, God did not send another Moses; He came himself in Jesus Christ.

Moses, we are told, was faithful in God's house as a servant. God's house is His people; He dwells among them and within them. "Christ was faithful over God's house as a son" (Heb. 3:6). He is the Creator and Redeemer of God's people. One greater than Moses came to rescue us from sin and to lead us to heaven.

The 10 terrible plagues that broke the back of Pharaoh's resistance were God's judgment "on all the gods of Egypt" (Exod. 12:12). And the death and resurrection of Jesus were a judgment upon Satan and the defeat of sin. Facing the Cross, Jesus said, "Now is the judgment of this world, now shall the ruler of this world be cast out" (John 12:31).

Before He went to the Cross, our Lord received a visit from Moses and Elijah. It took place at a mountain retreat where Jesus, as He prayed, was suddenly transfigured. His face and clothing became radiant with glory. Then the visitors appeared, and they conversed with Him about His coming death. They called that death an "exodus." Just as Moses led a gang of slaves to freedom through the parted waters of the Sea of Reeds, so Jesus Christ would lead a people out of sin into spiritual freedom through His atoning death.

I thank God that I am one of those freed slaves. Years ago I stood on a street corner, a slave to sin confronted with the claims of the gospel. The "ruler of this world" battled desperately to keep me shackled. I was helpless against the power of evil, but I trusted in Jesus Christ. He spoke His liberating word: "Let him go." And in the words of Charles Wesley's grand hymn,

My chains fell off; my heart was free.
I rose, went forth, and followed Thee.

In company with God's people I am making the journey to "a better country" (Heb. 11:16).

* * *

Whoever you are, whatever you have done, God wants to include you in His liberated people. He wants you to join the freedom march today. He is saying to the forces that have bound you in sin and guilt and misery, "Let my people go." You can never free yourself. Come to Him and be unshackled!

27

Deliverance Through Blood

Israel was enslaved. God heard their groans and cries and came to their rescue. He sent Moses to confront Pharaoh with His demand, "Let my people go" (Exod. 5:1). Stubborn Pharaoh refused, unwilling to part with cheap labor and even more unwilling to recognize higher authority.

To break the arrogant monarch's will, God had sent nine awful plagues upon Egypt. Now He was preparing the last and the worst plague—the death of the firstborn of all cattle and people.

To spare His people from that devastation, God, through Moses, gave them strange orders. Lambs were to be slain, "a lamb for a household" (12:3), and lamb's blood was to be sprinkled on the jambs and lintels of the doors of each house. To these slaves, hoping to flee the country, God gave a simple promise:

When I see the blood, I will pass over you (v. 13).

"At midnight the Lord smote all the first-born in the land of Egypt, from the first-born of Pharaoh who sat on his throne to the first-born of the captive who was in the dungeon, and all the first-born of the cattle" (v. 29). When God brings judgment upon sin, none are spared because their position is lofty, none because it is lowly. Throughout Egypt there was a plaintive lowing in the fields, an anguished sobbing in the homes. In palace, prison, and pasture death had come.

Though Egypt was devastated, Israel was spared. Not because they were righteous; not because they were deserving; not because they were slaves and had suffered enough already. And not because God was arbitrary or capricious, acting "without rhyme or reason." No, they were spared because they believed and obeyed God, placing the blood upon their doors. They were saved by the blood of the lambs.

That night a shaken Pharaoh summoned Moses and said, "Take your people and your flocks and go!" (cf. vv. 31-32). Throughout their history Israel has remembered that night. They celebrate the event each year in their Passover, their Seder, reciting anew the story of their blood-bought redemption from slavery.

In the course of Israel's history, Jesus came. And John the Baptizer pointed to Jesus Christ, exclaiming, "Behold, the Lamb of God, who takes away the sin of the world!" (John 1:29). Later, the apostle Paul proclaimed Jesus as the Redeemer, declaring, "Christ, our paschal lamb, has been sacrificed" (1 Cor. 5:7).

Sin is bondage, the cruelest form of slavery. It brutally perverts and corrupts life. To deliver us from sin, God sent Jesus Christ to become an atoning sacrifice. In His death He bore our sins, He endured our judgment, He purchased our freedom. Through His blood, therefore, we are saved—saved from a coming judgment more awesome than any plague that fell upon ancient Egypt. "Since, therefore, we are now justified by his blood, much more shall we be saved by him from the wrath of God" (Rom. 5:9). Saved from wrath—the wrath of God that is the final judgment upon evil.

The blood of the lamb was God's plan. Israel was not permitted to substitute any other Passover emblem. No one today can be delivered from the power and penalty of sin except through the blood of Jesus Christ.

You can hang your coat of arms upon the doorpost, but that will not save you. God is not impressed by the aristocracy of your ancestors. He knows that, whatever their positions and possessions, they were sinners just like you are.

You can hang your college diplomas upon the doorpost, but that will not save you. Education may civilize, but it cannot redeem from sin. The difference between heaven and hell is not a Ph.D.; it is the blood of Jesus Christ.

You can hang your balance sheet upon the doorpost, but that will not save you. Your money may buy privileges among men, but it cuts no ice with God. Rich and poor alike have sinned against Him, and their only escape from sin's doom is the blood of the Lamb.

You can hang your certificate of baptism upon the doorpost, but that will not save you. Thousands of people in every generation have joined the church who were never saved from sin. They went into the water dry sinners and came out wet sinners. There was not the slightest change in their moral lives. Divorced from true repentance and from faith in Jesus Christ, baptism is an empty ritual, and church membership a vain deception.

God alone can free the slaves of sin. God alone can redeem human life from bondage and invest it with eternal value. And He has chosen to do so through the atoning blood of Jesus Christ. His promise abides: "When I see the blood, I will pass over you." Where the blood is not applied, the result is judgment and destruction.

"Behold, the Lamb of God!" He is your only hope. Just before he died, Alfred Cookman, a noted Methodist preacher, said to his wife, "I am sweeping through the gates, washed in the blood of the Lamb!" The gates of new life, the gates of the city of God, open only to those who are cleansed from sin through the blood of Christ. Heaven's gates are hinged on Calvary's cross.

* * *

I know that scorn has been heaped upon it, but you will never face a more urgent question than the one expressed in a familiar gospel song: "Are you washed in the blood of the Lamb?"

28

The King Eternal

The children of Israel, fleeing from bondage in Egypt, passed through the Sea of Reeds on dry ground. God had graciously, miraculously parted the waters, allowing them to escape their enemies.

When the pursuing army of Egypt rushed into that same path of deliverance, the walls of water suddenly collapsed, overthrowing and destroying them.

Safe on the other side, the liberated slaves celebrated with songs and dancing, ascribing their deliverance to the goodness and power of God. Their victory song is recorded in Exodus 15, where God's "right hand" is exalted. Their fervent praise reached its climax in the shout,

The Lord will reign for ever and ever (v. 18).

The story of the Exodus introduces us to

I. POWERLESS GODS AND PERISHING CROWNS

Every pagan god was doomed before the wrath of the true and living God. The complex of events that made up the Exodus is described in Scripture as a judgment upon all the gods of Egypt. They were crushed in defeat, and the God of Israel was exalted in victory. Moses and his people sang, "Who is like thee, O Lord, among the gods? Who is like thee, majestic in holiness, terrible in glorious deeds, doing wonders?" (v. 11). The obvious answer was "No one."

In the centuries that followed, other idols were toppled, including the many legendary gods of Babylon, Greece, and Rome. And sooner or later the false gods of our own day will perish, but "The Lord will reign for ever and ever."

All earthly rulers mount shaking thrones and wear perishing crowns. Like haughty Pharaoh, they may strut across the map, commanding powerful armies and conquering many peoples, but their collapse and demise are sure. They are but flesh, and flesh is doomed to die and rot. As a court preacher once said at the funeral of a French king, "Only God is great." Ancient and modern Caesars alike, defying God and oppressing people, write their names upon water, but "The Lord will reign for ever and ever."

In contrast to these fragile thrones and passing kings, there is

II. AN ETERNAL KING, AN ENDURING KINGDOM

A King arose named Jesus Christ. He is a strange King who affirmed, "My kingship is not of this world" (John 18:36). In mad defiance of Him, "the kings of the earth set themselves, and the rulers [took] counsel together, against the Lord and his anointed, saying, 'Let us burst their bonds asunder, and cast their cords from us'" (Ps. 2:2-3). They gave Him a circlet of thorns for His crown and a bloody cross for His throne. As He died in fathomless anguish, they mocked in jubilation. But God raised Him from the dead and named Him "Lord of lords and King of kings" (Rev. 17:14). The risen Christ declared, "All authority in heaven and on earth has been given to me" (Matt. 28:18).

His subjects have been persecuted by petty despots in one century after another, in one country after another. Prison, torture, and death have failed to quench their loyalty and silence their praise. In this trembling earth they have received "a kingdom that cannot be shaken" (Heb. 12:28). Their King cannot be dethroned, and He will not abdicate. Therefore, they press on toward the divinely determined outcome of history: "The kingdom of the world has become the kingdom of our Lord and of his Christ, and he shall reign for ever and ever" (Rev. 11:15).

Today the Western world trembles before the nuclear might of Russia, fearing that power-mad and paranoid leaders might trigger a global holocaust. From within those Western nations shall arise an end-time dictator, the ultimate Antichrist, whose reign will dwarf all previous regimes for cruelty and carnage. But Holy Scripture looks beyond them all to the glorious return of Jesus Christ, and to the Kingdom whose righteousness and peace shall never be diminished. "The Lamb will conquer them, for he is Lord of lords and King of kings" (17:14).

Yes, Pharaohs come and go, kingdoms rise and fall, but "His kingdom is forever." To be a citizen of His kingdom is to possess a quenchless hope, an endless life. Upon the shore of the Sea of Reeds ancient Israel celebrated its freedom. And someday, in heaven, the ransomed of earth will "sing the song of Moses . . . and the song of the Lamb, saying, 'Great and wonderful are thy deeds, O Lord God the Almighty! Just and true are thy ways, O King of the ages!'" (15:3).

*　*　*

So I ask you the inevitable and important question—Are you serving the Lord Jesus Christ? Is He the King of your life today? When every earthly throne has toppled, when the last earthly empire has vanished, He will continue to reign. The rulers who enslave are doomed to extinction. The Lord who frees the slaves will reign throughout all ages. If you are linked with Him, you can share the joys and the glories of that eternal Kingdom! Get on the winning side!

29

The Healer

Let me share with you one of God's great promises to Israel. It is stated simply and boldly in these words:

I am the Lord, your healer (Exod. 15:26).

Does this promise abide? Can it be claimed by the Lord's people today? I believe that it can.

As we reflect upon this promise, it presents to us

I. THE HEALING CROSS

The promise occurs in a very interesting context. The children of Israel, having been delivered from Egyptian bondage, were beginning their trek through the wilderness. After three days of marching they were out of water. At a place called Marah they found some springs, but the water was unfit to drink. "It was bitter" (v. 23).

The people murmured against Moses, and Moses cried to the Lord. Responding to his prayers and to their needs, the Lord "showed him a tree" (v. 25). When that unidentified tree was cast into the waters, they became sweet and potable. Christian readers have seen in that tree a symbol of the cross of Jesus Christ, which turns death into life for those who believe in Him.

Saved by the supply of water that God had purified, Israel then received the promise of healing. Like all of God's promises, it was conditional.

> *If you will diligently hearken to the voice of the Lord your God, and do that which is right in his eyes, and give heed to his commandments and keep all his statutes, I will put none of the diseases upon you which I put upon the Egyptians; for I am the Lord, your healer* (v. 26).

Sickness may result from sin, and repentance must then precede healing. Sickness can be a divine judgment upon human sin, and only a turning from the evil that occasioned the judgment will bring the healing. When healing does occur, it signifies the willingness of God to forgive sins.

Other dramatic healings took place within Israel during their years in the wilderness. The strangest of them all was the healing of persons who had been stung by poisonous snakes. The Lord told Moses to fashion a serpent of bronze, mount it on a pole, and place it in the midst of the camp. Everyone who looked to it was healed and spared.

Centuries later Jesus Christ, referring to His coming death on the Cross, affirmed, "As Moses lifted up the serpent in the wilderness, so must the Son of man be lifted up, that whoever believes in him may have eternal life" (John 3:14-15). Healing issues from the atoning death of Christ. The One who died for our sins is

II. THE HEALING CHRIST

In the earthly ministry of Jesus Christ a large number of healings took place. All kinds of diseases, many of them long-standing cases, were healed by His words and His touch. He even raised the dead. These remarkable healings, according to Christ's own teaching, demonstrated His power on earth to forgive sins (e.g., Mark 2:10).

What Christ had done, His apostles continued to do. Invoking the power of His name, they healed the sick, while people looked on amazed and afraid.

"Jesus Christ is the same yesterday and today and for ever" (Heb. 13:8). The healing power of our Lord has not diminished with the passing of time. Possessing all authority in heaven and on earth, He can speak healing words and do healing deeds here and now. Faith and obedience are still the conditions of divine healing, and thousands of persons have been delivered at that holy junction where man's faith and God's power intersect.

Some teach that God always wills to heal the sick. According to these "faith healers," if you ask for healing and do not receive it, your continuing illness advertises your unbelief and sin. But "faith healers" also get sick and die, though thousands of their followers pray earnestly for their healing. Either they were mistaken in their teaching or backslidden in their hearts!

Some of God's choicest people, devout and sincere Christians, have not been healed despite volumes of earnest prayer. To brand all these sufferers as unbelieving or hypocritical persons is a rash and cruel judgment.

In a sense, all healing is from the Lord. His means of healing usually includes doctors, medicines, and therapies, but only He is the Giver and Restorer of life. And while He may employ medical science as an instrument of healing, He is also able to heal the sick immediately and directly by His word of power. A wonderful surgeon used to have me pray at the bedsides of his patients. When I asked him why, he replied, "We doctors know what we can do, but we never know what the Lord might do."

Every physical healing points to the grace and power of Christ to bring spiritual healing—the forgiveness of sins and the cleansing of our hearts. Spiritual healing is what ultimately matters. Sickness will not keep you from God and heaven, but sin can destroy body and soul in hell.

*   *   *

Have you taken your needs to the Great Physician? Let the Lord be your Healer today.

30

Heaven's Bread

Israel had escaped from Egypt. The slaves were freed by the hand of God. Now they are passing through the wilderness en route to Canaan, the Land of Promise. Before long their rations were exhausted, and the despairing people raged against Moses, accusing him of bringing them out of Egypt only to kill them with hunger.

The Lord intervened with the promise of "bread from heaven" (Exod. 16:4). In the morning the ground about their camp was covered with small, round, white particles that tasted "like wafers made with honey" (v. 31). They sampled it, then gathered it up, saying to one another, "What is it?" Moses gave them the only answer they were to receive:

> It is the bread which the Lord has given you to eat (v. 15).

I. THE GIFT OF GOD WAS BREAD FROM HEAVEN

By the miracle of the manna the children of Israel were sustained during 40 years of sojourning in the wilderness. Their daily bread was a gift of God, preserving the lives of undeserving and oft-complaining people.

All daily bread is a divine gift. It may not fall from heaven as did the manna. It may be a product of farm and bakery, trucked to stores and retailed to consumers, but it is still a merciful provision of divine love. Sun, rain, soil, and seed are not products of human ingenuity—they are bounties from God the Creator that supply us with strength for our journey through life. Every slice of bread we eat should prompt thanksgiving to God. Every piece of bread we share is a sign of the Father's love for us all, no matter how badly that sign may be misread by unbelieving men.

II. THE GIFT OF GOD WAS BREAD FOR LIVING

Manna was a sign pressed into the service of a greater truth. Centuries after Moses, Jesus Christ said, "I am the bread of life; he who comes to me shall not hunger. . . . I am the bread which came down from heaven" (John 6:35, 41). As our Savior from sin, Jesus Christ is the "living bread," the life-giving bread. He said, "I am the living bread which came down from heaven; if any one eats of this bread, he will live for ever" (v. 51). The fathers ate manna in the wilderness to sustain physical life. But the power of manna was limited, and sooner or later the eaters died. Jesus Christ is the Bread that gives and sustains spiritual life. Those who partake of Him receive spiritual life.

As "the bread of life," it was necessary for Christ to be broken. At the Last Supper with His followers "Jesus took bread, and blessed, and broke it, and gave it to the disciples and said, 'Take, eat; this is my body'" (Matt. 26:26). His body was broken at the Cross, where He died for our sins. That atoning death is our only hope of life. We feed on Him by believing in the merit and power of His death to ransom us from sin and reconcile us to God. Like the manna, Jesus is the gift of God to undeserving sinners, and He makes the difference between life and death.

III. THE GIFT OF GOD WAS BREAD IN ABUNDANCE

The manna is described as "bread to the full"—there was an adequate supply. Jesus Christ is bread to the full! His atoning death and risen life are sufficient for the salvation of all who believe in Him. "He is the atoning sacrifice for . . . the sins of the whole world" (1 John 2:2, NRSV). "He died for all" (2 Cor. 5:15). Whoever you are, whatever your sins, you were included in the saving death of our Lord.

The manna was supplied daily. Each man gathered it according to the day's need, some more, some less, depending on the size of one's family. "He that gathered much had nothing over, and he that gathered little had no lack" (Exod. 16:18). But the gift of manna could not be stockpiled for the future. Leaving any of it until the next day was forbidden. When some of the Israelites ignored that directive, the manna they kept until morning was found to be wormy and stinking.

Fellowship with God, which is eternal life, must be sustained on a day-by-day basis. Yesterday's bread will not energize today's march. Faith in Christ as a past event is not enough. Eternal life is given to those who "believe"—a continuous present-tense verb. Our Lord taught us to pray, "Give us this day our daily bread" (Matt. 6:11). The application is spiritual as well as physical.

The closing verses of Exodus 16 tell how a pot of manna was placed in the ark of the covenant, to be preserved as a memorial to the grace of God. Faith needs reminders. God's mercy to the fathers must be witnessed to the children in order that their own faith may be stimulated. This is the real significance of the crosses by which our church buildings are adorned. They point to Christ, our Redeemer, saying, "It is the bread which the Lord has given you to eat."

*   *   *

Jesus is the Bread of Life, given for all, given in abundance. In words of an old gospel song, "Come and dine."

31

The Smitten Rock

In the desert, out of water—that was the plight facing ancient Israel. They were fugitive slaves traveling a rugged road to freedom. In "the wilderness of Sin" a dire emergency arose: "there was no water for the people to drink" (Exod. 17:1).

They did what every band of trekkers has done in such circumstances: They blamed the trail boss. "The people found fault with Moses" (v. 2). You only brought us out of Egypt, they charged, to kill us with thirst! In their despair and anger they were almost ready to stone poor Moses.

You cannot reason with such people, and Moses did not try. He did a much wiser thing: "Moses cried to the Lord" (v. 4). And from the Lord he received these strange orders:

> Behold, I will stand before you there on the rock at Horeb; and you shall strike the rock, and water shall come out of it, that the people may drink (v. 6).

Moses obeyed the Lord and struck the rock. He had learned to obey without questioning the wisdom of strange ventures. From the smitten rock flowed an abundant stream of life-giving water. Undeserving, murmuring Israel slaked their thirst by the grace of God.

This old story has something to say to us. We can even find ourselves in the incident, for we are introduced to

I. A GRUMBLING PEOPLE

Upon the dramatic spot where this unusual episode took place, Moses conferred a pair of names. He called it Meribah, which means *strife*, for there the children of Israel contended against him, whining in unbelief, "Is the Lord among us or not?" And he called the place Massah, which means *proving* (v. 7), for there the Lord evidenced His love and power in the miraculous provision of water.

Centuries have passed, but human nature has not changed. Still today, people argue against the presence—and even the existence—of God because their circumstances are harsh and menacing. When new trials are encountered, old mercies are promptly forgotten. The cry of thankless hearts is always, "But what has God done for us lately?"

Over against this ungrateful people stood

II. A GRACIOUS GOD

God has not changed either. He still patiently endures our ingratitude, and He continues to sustain our lives with fresh expressions and measures of His goodness.

The God who stood before the rock at Horeb is the God who stood before the cross at Calvary. There His only-begotten Son was smitten to death, and from His atoning wounds flowed eternal life. "That Rock," wrote the apostle Paul, "was Christ" (1 Cor. 10:4, KJV).

At a religious feast in Jerusalem, Jesus stood up and cried out, "If any one thirst, let him come to me and drink. He who believes in me, as the scripture has said, 'Out of his heart shall flow rivers of living water.'" John adds this interpretive comment: "This he said about the Spirit, which those who believed in him were to receive; for as yet the Spirit had not been given, because Jesus was not yet glorified" (John 7:37-39).

In John's Gospel, Jesus begins to be glorified at His death on the Cross. The coming of the Holy Spirit, who is God's Living Water for the quenching of our spiritual thirst, awaited the smiting of the Rock. Pentecost, where the Holy Spirit was poured out in fullness, was linked to Calvary, where Jesus Christ was smitten and pierced in atoning death.

The water of life that Jesus gives cannot be earned or purchased by our works. All of us are just as undeserving as was that pack of grumbling, snarling ex-slaves who threatened Moses. Our deliverance from death, just as theirs, is the free gift of God.

Do you recall our Lord's first mention of the "living water"? He was conversing with a Samaritan woman whose reputation was sordid. She had been married five times, and now she was living with a man not her husband. To this adulteress our Lord revealed His Messiahship, and to her He spoke the gracious words,

> Whoever drinks of the water that I shall give him
> will never thirst; the water that I shall give him
> will become in him a spring of water welling up to
> eternal life (4:14).

This artesian well of life-giving, life-sustaining water is for all who will repent of their sins and believe in Jesus Christ.

Christ responds to our thirst, not to our merit. On the Cross He flung through tortured lips the cry, "I thirst" (John 19:28). From the Cross He provides the water of life that quenches our thirst for God eternally.

Horatius Bonar sang,

> I came to Jesus, and I drank
>   Of that life-giving stream;
> My thirst was quenched, my soul revived,
>   And now I live in Him.

Is that your song today? It can be! Jesus Christ, who was crucified for our sins and raised for our salvation, is the answer to our deep inward thirst for God.

32

The Ten Commandments

Exodus 20 contains the most influential piece of legislation ever recorded. It is commonly called the Ten Commandments. These brief moral directives became the foundation for the jurisprudence of Western civilization. Even when the commandments relating to man's relationship to God were ignored, those concerning man's relationship to man remained.

Despite their abiding popularity and influence, however, the famous "Ten Words" have often been badly misunderstood and sadly rejected. We do well to review them frequently, giving attention to their content.

We should begin where this chapter of Exodus begins:

And God spoke all these words (v. 1).

Here we are informed of

I. THE DIVINE CONTENT OF THE LAW

The Ten Commandments are laws given by God, not laws devised by men. They constitute divine revelation, not human legislation. They were covenant stipulations imposed upon Israel by the sovereign God, not negotiated by bargaining agents representing the nation.

Given by God, these laws are grounded in His nature, not in people's changing social conditions. They are moral absolutes, not moral relativities. They spell out, tersely and truly, how people must live to be fully human and to be rightly related to God. Unlike many aspects of Mosaic law, they transcend national boundaries and temporal restrictions. They speak God's mind for all people through all history.

Idolatry is wrong everywhere and for all time. Reverence for God is universally right. Every human life needs the rhythm of work and rest, observed in a manner that keeps the thought of God in the mind of man. Respect for parents is always crucial to strong families and enduring nations. The prohibition of murder, adultery, theft, and lying are more than bits of conventional morality; they are the very foundations of worthy and lasting human relationships. Covetousness is the root of those evil deeds that breach the laws of God, and its condemnation is demanded by a holy God and a loyal people.

Yes, what we have in the Ten Commandments is not moral etiquette subject to human revision. Rather, these laws constitute a faithful transcript of the will of God for the wisest and best ordering of human life.

It is important that we see also

II. THE GRACIOUS CONTENT OF THE LAW

We need to remember that the Ten Commandments are laws given in the context of grace. "And God spoke all these words, saying, 'I am the Lord your God, who brought you out of the land of Egypt, out of the house of bondage'"

(Exod. 20:1-2). God prefaced His moral demands with a reminder of the Exodus. These laws were given to a people already redeemed from slavery by the love and power of God. He had graciously taken them to be His people, motivated not by their worth but solely by His love. Law was not given as a means by which man could earn God's favor. Law was given to guide the lives of a people who were already recipients of that favor. They were not saved by keeping the law; they were given the law as a redeemed people.

If our salvation from sin and death rested upon our lawkeeping, our hearts would be prisoned forever in despair. "All have sinned," because "the mind that is set on the flesh is hostile to God; it does not submit to God's law, indeed it cannot" (Rom. 3:23; 8:7). Man is a rebel against God. He is inwardly twisted out of joint with God's will, and he gives outward expression to that inward twist by his repeated transgressions. He can no more gain favor with God by keeping the Ten Commandments than he can lift himself over a fence by tugging at the laces of his boots.

God saves us, not according to our righteousness, but according to His mercy. We are saved by grace, not by works; by faith in Christ, not by doing good.

The law defines sin and causes us to despair of being saved by our moral efforts. But the context of the Ten Commandments supplies us with hope in the face of broken law. It proclaims a gracious Redeemer, a God who rescues sinful, guilty, unworthy people from their bondage because His name and nature is love.

This Redeemer-God not only inscribes His law upon tablets of stone and pages of Scripture; He writes them upon the hearts of His forgiven, believing people, furnishing them with an inward power for obedience. "I will put my laws on their hearts, and write them on their minds" (Heb. 10:16).

His redeemed community keeps the law, not to earn His favor, but to express their gratitude for the mercy already shown to them. Incorrectly viewed, law becomes the enemy of grace. Seen correctly, law is the servant of grace.

The Ten Commandments stand as an everlasting reminder that God saves us by His grace and guides us by His law.

33

The Moral Minority

You shall not follow a multitude to do evil
(Exod. 23:2).

That was God's law for ancient Israel, and that is His word to modern Christians. Stand for the right if you have to stand alone! Indeed, stand for the right even if you get knocked down and run over.

What is right? What is wrong? How can we decide? Let's take a vote—that's the good old democratic way! But that is not the biblical way. Scripture does not teach consensus ethics. God does not leave decisions on moral issues to congresses or courts. Right and wrong are His decisions, and they are grounded in His nature, not in our culture.

The text recognizes

I. THE MENACING MAJORITY

Fifty million Frenchmen can be wrong. "Right is right if no one does it; wrong is wrong if everyone does it." The majority may rule now, but God will be the final Judge of our lives. Before Him we cannot excuse our sins by pointing to the crowds.

Peer group pressure is subtle and powerful. Every normal person craves acceptance. No one wants to be an oddball or an outcast. To purchase the favor of our peers at the cost of our souls, however, is a ruinous bargain. To be rejected by the crowd hurts deeply, but that is a small price to pay for acceptance with God. "What does it profit a man, to gain the whole world and forfeit his life?" (Mark 8:36).

At one time "all the people" of Israel were cavorting in an idolatrous orgy before a golden calf. Against them stood one man, clutching in his hands the law of God, and denouncing in hot anger their inexcusable evildoing. The conscience of Moses was bound to the Word of God. He would not follow a multitude to do evil.

The Book of Proverbs says, "In an abundance of counselors there is safety" (11:14; see also 24:6). But those proverbs presuppose that the counselors are men committed to "the way of the Lord," men for whom "the fear of the Lord is the beginning of wisdom" (9:10). Nowhere does the Bible allow the opinion of a majority to become an excuse for doing wrong. Where moral values are concerned, our "multitude of counsellors" (11:14, KJV) should be the 66 books of the Bible, not the consensus of men and women who reject Jesus Christ and substitute their decisions for the Lord's commandments.

The text recognizes, therefore,

II. THE MORAL MINORITY

The Lord Jesus taught His followers to reject popular notions and live as a moral minority. He commanded,

> *Enter by the narrow gate, for the gate is wide and the way is easy, that leads to destruction, and those who enter by it are many. For the gate is narrow and the way is hard, that leads to life, and those who find it are few* (Matt. 7:13-14).

Paul declared that "the world did not know God through wisdom" (1 Cor. 1:21). That is just as true of the world's moral wisdom as its philosophical wisdom.

Courage is demanded of all who refuse to go along with the crowd in its evildoing. Such dissenters may become the victims of the world's enmity against God. Arrogant sinners who are playing God do not take kindly the rejection of their moral pronouncements. To question their right to do wrong may bring wrath down upon the questioners. Daniel found it so and was flung into a den of lions for daring to pray to the true and living God.

God locked the jaws of those lions, but He does not always spare His brave and lonely covenant-keepers. In the early days of the Church, it was Stephen against the Sanhedrin, and when they could not silence his preaching, they stoned him to death. In his dying moments he "saw the glory of God, and Jesus standing at the right hand of God" (Acts 7:55). It is better to die at peace with God than to live with an outraged conscience.

Who can measure the destruction that has resulted from following the crowd? I recall a young man who visited a sleazy bar with some friends. He did not really want to go, but he lacked the courage to risk their ridicule and rejection. A fight broke out, and in the ensuing melee he was knifed in the stomach. The doctor who patched him up said, "It looked like someone had stuck a knife in his side and tried to walk around him without pulling it out." For days he lingered at the brink of death, and the recovery of his health and strength required months of time. Even so, he was more fortunate than many have been in similar situations.

Majority opinion and popular custom do not determine what is right and wrong. The Christian has one question to ask of any proposed action: What does God say in His Word? Whatever the majority may think, the believer prefers to be bound to the will of God in life and death!

34

The Golden Calf

The children of Israel were camped at the foot of Mount Sinai. Moses had climbed the mountain, called to its summit by the Lord, there to receive the law by which the people were to be governed.

After 40 days in that glorious Presence, he returned to the camp. A horrible sight greeted him. The people were singing and dancing before a golden calf. Worse yet, their idolatrous orgy was being led by Aaron, older brother of Moses and high priest of Israel.

Grieved and angry, Moses demanded an accounting. The response of Aaron is a classic for absurdity. He blamed the whole affair on the people, insisting that they were "set on evil." They had demanded gods to lead them. Aaron had taken donations of gold jewelry from them and had forged the idol from those gifts. Lamely, he explained to Moses,

> *I threw it into the fire, and there came out this calf* (Exod. 32:24).

Two characters in contrast meet us here. The first is

I. A LYING PRIEST

Aaron's pathetic excuse was a lie. The calf did not emerge from the flames. Aaron "fashioned it with a graving tool" (v. 4), deliberately violating God's first and second commandments for Israel's life.

Idols never just happen. They are fashioned by human hands responding to human wills. God created man, and man has created gods. John Calvin described the human mind as a "perpetual manufactory of idols." Unwilling to serve God who made them, men have devised gods to please themselves. In turn, they have become the tragic slaves of their made-to-order gods.

Idolatry does not just happen. It results from a deliberate refusal to worship the true God, who is revealed in Jesus Christ, and to whom the Bible bears witness. To give anyone or anything the place in your life that God should have is idolatrous. Idolatry fills the vacuum created by the rejection of our Creator and Redeemer. When He is spurned, a creature powerless to redeem takes His place.

Israel's idol, on this occasion, was a golden calf. Your idol may be an automobile, a television set, or a piece of real estate. The state may become a false god, or the church, or the family. Your idolatrous rituals may occur in a sports arena. Unless God has first place in your life, you have an idol, and you engage in idolatry.

Recurrent lapses into idolatry marred the history of God's covenant people, Israel. Such lapses are a constant threat to His new covenant people, the church. For good reason, the apostle John wrote to Christians, "Little children, keep yourselves from idols" (1 John 5:21). Just before he penned this plea, he wrote,

> We know that the Son of God has come and has
> given us understanding, to know him who is true;
> and we are in him who is true, in his Son Jesus
> Christ. This is the true God and eternal life (v. 20).

135

Knowing the true God, revealed in the Savior Jesus Christ, is not something we can take for granted. Those who are "in him" must guard constantly against the idols of a surrounding culture.

Just as idolatry does not just happen, so the worship of and service of the true God never occurs automatically or incidentally. Jesus said, "Seek first his kingdom" (Matt. 6:33). We must deliberately put God first, diligently place our lives under His rule, yield our wills to His will. "Thy will be done" (v. 10) must be our daily prayer and daily practice.

So there, in all his shame, stood a lying priest. And already we have anticipated the second character. In severe contrast to that lying priest and his dead idol, we confront

II. A LIVING GOD

The golden calf was a miserable substitute for the God who plagued Egypt, who opened the Sea of Reeds, who rained bread from heaven when the people hungered, who poured water from a smitten rock when they thirsted. Why would anyone prefer an impotent idol to such a God?

The answer lies in the blinding and binding power of sin. Sinful man wants a god in his own image. Such a god will not condemn his sins, will not disturb his conscience, will not threaten his existence. The true and living God cannot be manipulated, cannot be deceived, cannot be bribed. God cannot be made the tool of priests or monarchs. He will not justify oppression. He demands truth, justice, and holiness. Unable or unwilling to accept these demands, men turn to gods of their own making.

The true God would be our doom if He were not merciful and forgiving as well as just and holy. He forgave His ancient people again and again when they repented of their sins and forsook their idols. And He forgives today those who turn from their wicked ways and believe in Jesus Christ, His Son and our Savior.

The living God is the only hope of a dying race. A golden calf is powerless to save. According to the Bible, an idol is nothing. The one who rejects God to serve idols is sacrificing everything to gain nothing. The one who rejects idols to serve God is losing nothing and gaining everything!

"Choose this day whom you will serve" (Josh. 24:15).

35

Face-to-face with God

In all the rich materials that record the life and work of Moses, this passage is the most outstanding:

> *Thus the Lord used to speak to Moses face to face,*
> *as a man speaks to his friend* (Exod. 33:11).

Two factors especially enter into the greatness of Moses. The first is this:

I. MOSES WAS A MAN WHO LIVED CLOSE TO GOD

Moses entered into a deep, personal communion with God, a friendship with the Divine that filled his life with glory and beauty.

Throughout the record of his career these words occur over and over again: "The Lord said to Moses, Say to the people of Israel . . ." The people of Israel had a secondhand experience of God because of their defiant hearts and dull spirits. Moses enjoyed a firsthand experience of God because he was yielded, obedient, and trusting.

"Do you know Jesus?" a little boy was asked by his playmate.

"Sure I do," he responded. "We learn all about Him at church."

"No, no. That's not what I mean. Do you know Him to talk to and walk with?"

That is how Moses knew God.

It is one thing to know *about* God, but fellowship is not created by a course in doctrine. What really counts is knowing Him as one knows a friend, having personal communion with Him. Do you know God?

This firsthand acquaintance with God never happens accidentally. Moses craved fellowship with God. His heart yearned for God as the panting deer yearns for water. Two verses beyond our text we hear Moses say to God, "Show me now thy ways, that I may know thee and find favor in thy sight" (v. 13). And seven verses beyond the text we hear Moses cry out, "I pray thee, show me thy glory" (v. 18).

When a man's heart is consumed with thirst to know the grace and glory of God, then God will be pleased to make himself known in gracious, glorious, intimate, and saving ways.

Moses towered over his contemporaries in many ways. No greater man arose in Israel's history until Jesus came. But the most impressive feature of Moses' life was his friendship with God. When the gallant lawgiver died, someone added to the record these words: "And there has not arisen a prophet since in Israel like Moses, whom the Lord knew face to face" (Deut. 34:10).

There is a second dimension to the greatness of Moses, and it is closely linked to the first.

II. MOSES WAS A MAN WHO LIVED CLOSE TO HIS PEOPLE

At times they wearied him to the point of exasperation. They chafed under his leadership. They constantly blamed him when the going was rough. There were defiant challenges to his authority, even from his family. When anything went wrong, they chose him immediately for a scapegoat. No man ever championed and served a more contrary, less grateful people than did Moses. Once the burden of leadership weighed so heavily upon him that Moses actually begged God to kill him (see Num. 11:10-15).

And yet, the love and care of Moses for Israel never failed. On two occasions the wrath of God burned against the people because of their idolatry and unbelief. God threatened to disinherit them and call from the loins of Moses a greater and mightier nation. "Let me alone," said the Lord, "that my wrath may burn hot against them and I may consume them, but of you I will make a great nation" (Exod. 32:10; see also Num. 14:12).

But Moses would not let God alone. He stepped into the breach as an intercessor, pleading for the pardon of the people. If the people could not be forgiven, Moses begged to be blotted out himself. Here was a man who identified himself completely with an undeserving people. And God hearkened to Moses' prayer! He pardoned His people and continued to be with them.

When Moses was facing death, his concern was still the people. He urged the Lord to name his successor, "that the congregation of the Lord may not be as sheep which have no shepherd" (Num. 27:17). To the very last, Moses had a shepherd's heart.

Israel would not see a man like him again until Jesus came and said, "I am the good shepherd. The good shepherd lays down his life for the sheep" (John 10:11). And when Jesus laid down His life for us sinners, He prayed from the Cross, "Father, forgive them" (Luke 23:34).

* * *

A man of God, a man of the people—that was Moses. Is that true of you? Is that true of me? May God give such leaders to His Church for these perilous days of march and warfare!

36

God's Glory Revealed

Moses was a man who walked with God. The most impressive facet of his life was his deep communion with the Almighty. Scripture tells us that "the Lord used to speak to Moses face to face, as a man speaks to his friend" (Exod. 33:11).

During one of their conversations Moses became a spokesman for the deepest desire of the human heart. He cried out to God,

I pray thee, show me thy glory (v. 18).

Above everything else,

I. MAN HUNGERS TO KNOW GOD

Moses wanted to know exactly what God is like. He craved the fullest possible knowledge of the Eternal. And Moses knew that God cannot be discovered by our probing and groping. Whatever knowledge of God we possess must come from divine revelation, God's gracious self-disclosure.

In response to the prayer of Moses, God said, "You cannot see my face; for man shall not see me and live" (v. 20). The utter glory of God, suddenly confronting man, would destroy him. Frail, sinful human beings would be blinded and dissolved by the unutterable splendor of God.

Nevertheless, God accommodated himself to the plea of His friend. He placed Moses in the cleft of the rock, and when God passed by, the shadowed lawgiver beheld what Scripture quaintly calls God's "back." Moses glimpsed the receding glory of God and heard Him proclaiming His name: "The Lord, the Lord, a God merciful and gracious, slow to anger, and abounding in steadfast love and faithfulness" (34:6). What a glorious moment that was for Moses! It is not surprising that he "made haste to bow his head toward the earth, and worshiped" (v. 8).

"Show me thy glory"! The cry arises from the Old Testament—and from the heart of every person who awakens spiritually. We hunger to know God.

II. GOD SATISFIES MAN'S HUNGER IN CHRIST

"We have beheld his glory" (John 1:14)! This is the daring witness of the New Testament, a witness given by men who looked upon Jesus Christ.

Speaking of Christ, confessing Him as the eternal Word of God who entered history as a man, the Gospel of John declares,

> The Word became flesh and dwelt among us, full of grace and truth; we have beheld his glory, glory as of the only Son from the Father. . . . No one has ever seen God; the only Son, who is in the bosom of the Father, he has made him known (vv. 14, 18).

The human life of Jesus Christ is a faithful transcript of the nature of God. In Jesus Christ, God has revealed himself as truly and fully as possible to mankind. Jesus Christ is the answer to our cry for a knowledge of the glory of God.

This is precisely how Jesus understood himself. One of His disciples said, "Show us the Father, and we shall be satisfied" (14:8). Philip's plea was an echo of the words of Moses. And the response of Jesus was, "He who has seen me has seen the Father" (v. 9).

The apostle Paul proclaimed this same truth. To the church at Corinth he wrote,

> The God who said, "Let light shine out of darkness,"
> . . . has shone in our hearts to give the light of the
> knowledge of the glory of God in the face of Jesus
> Christ (2 Cor. 4:6, NRSV).

The Incarnation was both veiling and unveiling, veiling in order to vision. As Charles Wesley wrote, "Veiled in flesh the Godhead see."

God's glory is revealed in the human life of Christ. As Christ "went about doing good and healing all that were oppressed by the devil" (Acts 10:38), the glory of God's love, mercy, truth, justice, and holiness were conspicuously demonstrated. By the words and deeds of Jesus people came to a knowledge of the glory of God.

We are now dependent upon the Bible for our knowledge of God in Christ. As we read of Christ in its pages, the Holy Spirit illumines our hearts, enabling us to see Christ as more than a strange rabbi, healer, or martyr. We discover in Him the God of the Exodus, the God of Sinai, the God who redeems from bondage and legislates for freedom. We discover in Him the God who hates sin but loves the sinner, the God who is willing to save and able to keep.

"God was in Christ, reconciling the world unto himself" (2 Cor. 5:19, KJV). The life and death and resurrection of Jesus were a flaming forth of the glory of God's forgiving, cleansing, renewing love. In Jesus Christ we behold the God who champions the poor, the widow, the orphan, and the oppressed. We see in Him the God who cares for all who sin, who suffer, and who sorrow.

What a high and holy moment occurred on the Mount of Transfiguration when the flesh, and even the clothing, of Jesus became radiant with an unearthly glory—and Moses appeared to converse with Him! And what a great moment we shall know, we who follow the Christ of whom Scripture speaks, when we shall stand before Him, "face to face in all His glory."

To be human is to hunger for God. God reveals himself in Jesus Christ. Christ is the answer to our deepest longing and need.

"Show me thy glory"!

"We have beheld his glory"!

"The glory of God in the face of Jesus Christ"!